Other Books by Madison Meadows

Stringing Beads: Making a Beautiful Life Moment by Moment, Intro

Stringing Beads: Making a Beautiful Life Moment by Moment I

Stringing Beads: Making a Beautiful Life Moment by Moment II

Shedding the Wife
a spiritual journey through divorce

Madison Meadows

iv

Dedication

to my mom Sue
who's warm heart
and loving support
kept me
moving forward
through my
dark night of the soul

Disclaimer:

I must warn you Reader, that what you are about to read in the following pages may not sit well with you. My divorce was messy and my emotions raw. Read at your own risk of being offended.

I have tried to recreate events, locales, and conversations from my memories of them. I have changed plenty of details in some instances like names of individuals and physical descriptions, places, and occupations to protect the privacy of individuals.

Contents

x

The Split

This place is a dream. Only a sleeper considers it real. Then death comes like dawn, and you wake up laughing at what you thought was your grief. -Rumi

Introduction

Every man's life is a fairytale written by God's finger. -Anderson

You cannot move through anger and hatred without first recognizing this within yourself. The feelings of rage I had towards my husband and the woman he left me for consumed me.

All the yoga and meditation that I have done for the past twenty years could not carve out the darkness that blinded me. I only knew that I must give myself time to heal, permission to feel the extreme lows, and courage to explore the source of my anger. I started by asking myself, "When did I begin feeling this way in my marriage with Sam?"

Looking back, I felt abandoned by Sam a long time ago. Throughout our marriage, it began to feel that he resented me for exploring my inner life. I was a stay at home mom running the family business. I prioritized my family and God in my daily life. I set time aside every day for yoga, meditation, and writing. But the day did come when Sam would make sharp comments like, "What have you been doing all day?"

His callousness and snide remarks made me feel inferior to him. I quickly learned to put away the book I was reading or my journal as soon as I heard him pull into the driveway. I wanted to avoid any confrontation at all cost. So then why did I stay? After all, this wouldn't be the first time he cheated on me either.

Like any good woman who loves God and my family, I wanted what was best for my children. Sam has always been a good father and provider. And children need fathers as role models and emotional stability. So, I saw my unhappiness as a small price to pay. I also told myself that God doesn't make mistakes. Seeing as I've done all the right things in life as a wife and as a woman wanting to deepen my relationship with God, surely this is His doing.

Like the Casting Crowns song, *Slow Fade*, reminds me that it's important to guard your thoughts. "*It's a slow fade when you give yourself away. It's a slow fade when black and white turn to gray and thoughts invade, choices are made, a price will be paid when you give yourself away. People never crumble in a day. Daddies never crumble in a day. Families never crumble in a day."*

I know no other way to dissolve the anger in me other than to give it a voice. Through writing, I am releasing it, and slowly it loses its power over me. I feel I am being true to my feelings and doing so in a very authentic way. Many will not agree with my method, and some will be offended by my words. But I am not here to win your approval, but to honor the feelings within me during the most traumatic time in my life. I only hope other women will find their voice and courage to examine and explore what their role is in their marriage and ask questions like, *Am I being treated as an equal? Is my reality being validated by my partner?*

By keeping true to my feelings, I've decided to piece together the events as they happened in chronological order starting with, *The Split*, then, *The Dreams* and lastly, *The Poetry*. Daily I wrote in my journal my feelings, thoughts, and dreams. I feel my reader will see a progression (and relapse) of my inner state by staying true to the timeline of events and the thoughts that were inside my head at the time.

I cannot stress enough the value of dream work and prayer during my divorce. The guidance I got from my dreams helped me make better choices for myself and avoid many pitfalls along the way. The prayers that I offered *Spirit,* in my quiet surrender, I believe sent the right people in my life to help me get through my divorce. God is great!

The Other Woman

Let no one say when he is tempted, "I am tempted by God"; for God cannot be tempted with evil and he himself tempts no one, but each person is tempted when he is lured and enticed by his own desire. James 1:13-14

It is January in Tucson, the coldest month of the year here. Two weeks ago, my husband, Sam, asked for a separation and moved out. I was suspicious that he was having an affair. Yes, our marriage was having problems, but as a woman, my gut told me that there was another woman. I had been badgering him, asking, "Is there another woman?"

His reply was, "No M there is no one else." We have just grown apart, and you're just not into me anymore."

It is 10:30 pm on a Monday. I am waiting for Sam to bring our son home. He was supposed to have him back at 9 pm. I pace back and forth in my living room looking at the clock every five minutes. Finally, I hear the sound of my minivan. I slip on my Converse not caring that I am in my nightgown and rush to go out front to confront Sam. I think it's odd he didn't pull in the driveway and instead is parked out front on the street with the engine still running.

At first glance, I notice a woman, with long black hair wearing a baseball cap driving my minivan. My husband and son step out of the minivan. A tidal wave of emotion suddenly hits me with the realization that my husband is cheating. I yell at him, "What the fuck? You lying son of a bitch!"

I feel myself fade into the background; my heart is pounding; I can't see straight. The past two decades with Sam flash through my mind: when we dated, moving into his house, him proposing to me, our wedding day, and the birth of our children.

It happened so fast. I opened the driver's side door, reached in, and grabbed the woman's stringy hair and pulled as hard as I could.

My husband rushes between us and yells, "Stop, stop, let go M!"

The woman screams, "Get her off of me!"

All my neighbors are inside and don't respond to the noise in the street. I looked at my son. He is visibly shaking and crying. He is in shock. I let go of the woman's hair out of fatigue. My husband says with a commanding voice, "Get inside!"

I am shaking uncontrollably. What have I done? My thoughts go to my son who witnessed his mother losing it. He is scarred for life.

My Goodbye Letter

I couldn't sleep that night. So, I wrote a letter to Sam. It was just the beginning of my nightmare, but I didn't know that at the time.

Sam,

Just two weeks ago you asked for a separation, and you moved out. In a single moment last night, I saw our last twenty years flash before my eyes. I saw when we were dating, and I lived with Angel. You'd come to hang out with me to watch X Files, and she'd make her famous meatloaf and mash potatoes. I saw the day you proposed with the ring hidden in the Mexican food take-out. I saw our wedding day in your dad's backyard. I saw the day our son was born, you cried. I saw our place in Dearing Park, and that day our son got lost in the forest.

I saw the day our daughter was born and how protective you were when I brought her home because we had the flu. I saw all the times we spent with our kids at K and N's just hanging out while our kids played. I saw the trip to Disneyland we took with your dad and stepmom. I saw our vacation to California with J and the fun we had on the beach. I saw all the holidays and birthdays we spent with our families. But in a moment my heart was ripped out of my chest.

I know we have been falling apart. It was ten years ago when we went through your affair with B. We survived. But this time I know we can't fix it. I have been up all night crying. I am in a lot of pain. I am sorry for my part in us falling apart. You are a good father, and the children need you more now than ever. Please be there for them during this transition. Please do the right thing, if not for me, for them. I will always love you. I need time to heal.

Please don't humiliate me in front of our neighbors and friends and bring that woman around until the divorce is final; I would greatly appreciate it. I do want us to try and get along as best as possible for the sake of the kids. I will have to work through my emotions that I am feeling right now. You broke my heart. I now know it is best if we both move on. Was the last twenty years all that bad? I would do it all over again. I wouldn't change a thing. Please stay focused in life with what's important, put your children first. That's all I ask. May you find what you're looking for and God bless you.

M

The Phone Call

A week before this incidence, a friend of mine had called me to tell me that she saw my husband at Hooters with another woman. She told me the woman's name and that they had gone to school together. For months my husband had been staying out late or not coming home at all. Often, he said, "I am working late and meeting clients after hours. We have some beers. I shouldn't drive. I will just crash on my partner's couch."

I checked my husband's Facebook and scrolled through his Friends. I found the woman my friend had described. I messaged her to call me, and to my surprise she did.

Me: Hello, this is M.

Her: This is Namah.

Me: I just want to know are you having an affair with my husband?

Her: No, I'm not having an affair with your husband. Sam and I are just friends. I've known him since we were kids. I'm currently in a relationship with a great guy.

13

Me: Thanks for calling me. For months I have asked Sam to introduce me to all his friends at Hooters. I see the stupid pics that his partner posts with Sam and read comments like, *Threesome? Or Hot!* And here I am at home with our children taking care of them. Since you are friends with him, I figured I could vent. I think it's been totally inappropriate.

Her: I told Sam that I would like to meet you. I told Sam this weekend would work for me if that works for you?

Me: That would be great. Saturday works for me.

Her: I will talk to Sam and get back to you.

(End of the first phone call, the beginning of the second.)

Her: Hi M. Sam said he was picking the kids up tomorrow. I suggested that I went with him. We could do the meet and greet then.

Me: Why would you come with him to meet my kids at my house and not somewhere without the kids? That doesn't sound like just friends.

Her: It's quite the opposite. I didn't see an issue with me taking a ride with Sam to pick up the kids. I was planning on taking my daughter along for the ride. I'm not sure what you're hoping to gain from the meeting. The only thing that you will see is a friendship between two grown adults. Sam is not the only male friend that I have. My boyfriend is accepting to mine and Sam's friendship and with all my other friendships. He was the one who suggested me to go along with Sam to pick up the kids.

Me: Good, then bring your boyfriend too so I can meet him.

Her: I would love to, but unfortunately he is out of town on business. Not to mention he wouldn't come along. He thinks this whole thing is crazy. He doesn't do drama. He wants nothing to do with this. He is being supportive of my decision to meet you but doesn't agree with it. We respect each other's feelings. He is a lot like Donald Trump. My favorite quality of his.

Me: Okay, just pick some other place to meet.

Her: What is your reason for wanting to meet me? This is your idea. I'm just going along with it. Where would you like to meet? Would you like to meet for lunch?

Me: Sure, how about Applebee's? I just want to clear the air.

Her: Okay, I will see you then.

Needless to say, when I hung up the phone, I was very confused by our conversation. But she likens her boyfriend to Donald Trump, so that explains it all!

My Confession

Before I go any further and share my memories of my marriage and thoughts during my messy divorce, I first have to confess that for the past twenty years I have loved two men.

When I first heard about Sam's friend, Adam, I was living with Sam's ex-wife Jordan. Jordan kept on bringing up this man that I need to meet and how perfect we would be together. She told me all about him- how he was an EMT and spent a winter backpacking through India, Nepal, and Pakistan. During his travels, he climbed Mount Everest, watched a body burn on the Ganges River, and listened to the Dahli Lama. I was very intrigued, and I did want to meet Adam. I didn't even realize it right away, but my heart was already racing towards this mysterious, unknown man.

Jordan eventually moved out of the apartment we shared. Her ex-husband, Sam, moved in and for six months we cohabitated. After that, Sam rented a room from a friend, and I got an apartment with my friend Angel. We exchanged phone numbers and kept in touch. Sam was so easy to be with. I could just be myself around him. We became inseparable.

Then the day came when his friend came into town for a visit. I remember that day driving over to Sam's in my old Dodge Ram. I was nervous and secretly hoped that there would be no connection with this man. I was in a committed relationship with Sam and didn't want any complications.

When I walked into Sam's house, my heart was pounding so loud I could hear my heartbeat and my palms were sweaty. Adam and Sam were in the kitchen casually hanging out. At first glance, I noticed that I registered nothing- I felt nothing, nothing at all. I was so relieved that I took a deep breath. I could finally put to rest all the daydreams I had of this man.

Shortly after that encounter Sam and I moved in together. He owned a house with his first wife. He had a renter in it during his divorce. Sam was now ready to move back in and start a new life with me. I was excited. This was my first house with a partner. Sam and I painted, recarpeted, landscaped, and remodeled the kitchen and bathroom to our liking. It felt like a real home, the home I had always longed for.

One day Sam was gone to work. I was home reading a magazine. I was in my bedroom when I heard a knock on the door. I wasn't expecting anyone. It was the middle of the day. I remember it being the end of summer early fall and that I was wearing jeans.

I opened the door and standing before me was Adam. I felt heaven open up, and the stars descend when I looked into his eyes. My soul instantly recognized his soul. I had heard the expression *'love at first sight'* but never believed such a thing existed. But here I was caught up in a moment that can only be described as pure ecstasy. And all I could say was, "Would you like a beer?"

That encounter changed the course of my life. I was already dedicated to a spiritual path, and now I was aware of a presence that existed beyond space and time that connected my heart to this man's heart.

Adam went on to become the catalyst for my spiritual longing for God. He was the bridge that connected me to the Divine directly. The love I felt for this man consumed my soul and took me on an inward, upward journey into higher spiritual realms, for what would become, the next twenty years.

Going through my divorce with Sam, I've asked myself, *did I marry Sam to keep his friend close to me?* Truthfully, I can say no. I married Sam because I loved him and wanted to spend the rest of my life with him. But there is a part of me that liked the idea of knowing Adam would always be nearby.

Adam is an ongoing subject during our divorce. Sam blames me for his infidelities. He complains that I wasn't emotionally available to him because I loved another man, thereby throwing him into the arms of other women.

Over the years I prayed that God would work a miracle in my husband's heart. I won't apologize for loving another man. I never acted on my feelings. I have never spoken to this man about that day. Over the years I have had many dreams of Adam. They have inspired my creative writing and deepened my relationship with God. My sister-in-law describes it in this way; she said, "You committed manslaughter M. Sam committed first-degree murder."

Blood Soaked Tears

I waited 'til my children were gone to have my breakdown. It was the first weekend they'd be going with Sam to Namah's house- where Sam now lives.

I poured a hot bath, put on my Youtube playlist- which consists of Rob Thomas *Ever The Same* and *Someday*, Alison Krauss *Down To The River to Pray*, Lifehouse *Broken* and *Storm*, Ed Sheeran *Photograph*, Dido *White Flag*, and Casting Crowns *Broken*. I then entered into a hole that was deep, empty, and pitch black. I felt like a plastic doll- hollow inside. What was happening to me was so unreal.

The helpless, abandoned little girl emerged and screamed out- cursing, paralyzed in fear. *Would I make it through the night?* I wondered. *Or would I drown in this bathtub of blood-soaked tears?*

Hostage Trade-Off

During the week my kids are with me. On Fridays, after school, Sam comes to get them. He will park on the street and come up to the door. Why he doesn't pull into the driveway is beyond me.

The kids are told to pack their bags and to hurry. Sam lives forty-five minutes away on the other side of town. Traffic can get bad during rush hour.

So, like a hostage trade-off, the kids march out front to Sam's truck with overnight bags in hand. My daughter still sleeps with her teddy bear, so Teddy is part of the trade-off. I hug them one last time and tell them, "Mommy loves you."

Sam drives off. I then go into the house and ball my eyes out.

A Girl's Best Friend

I should feel guilty, but I don't. A part of me needed to see if there was anything left between Sam and me. I'm sure Sam did take full advantage of me in my vulnerable state. I did miss him, and sex with Sam was always satisfying.

Afterward, a part of me did regret it. I was worried about getting an STD, and I also felt demoralized by the action. I felt like the adulterous. It was a rush during the act, but that feeling quickly wore off. So, I made a promise to myself; I would never allow that to happen again.

So, the next time I went to the store I got an eight-pack of AA batteries. From that moment on my vibrator has become my lover and best friend.

Victoria's Secret

I was at the ball game watching my son play baseball. It happened to be the weekend after Valentine's Day. I had to retrieve something out of Sam's truck, and that's when I saw it. The pink Victoria's Secret bag there on the floorboard.

I wondered did Sam intend to leave it there? Or did she hope I would discover it and get insanely jealous? I have yet to see Namah in the daylight. My friends have described her as a Rumer Willis look-a-like.

Of course, my friends also told me she's not as pretty as me. This makes me feel only a little better. I did have a dream of her. In the dream, she was having sex with Sam. Seeing the Victoria's Secret bag made me think of that dream. I didn't want those uninvited images in my head!

Wednesday

With Sam gone, so are all the vehicles we had accumulated together. Our driveway looked like a parking lot. My classic 1970 Chevelle Sam gave to me after his first affair now is parked at Namah's house. Sam's two-door chopped '50 Chevy is stored in my garage out back and does not run. Sam kept his red 2012 Chevy Silverado that he uses for work. The old 4 Runner that I used as a backup vehicle, Sam sold to our neighbor. Every day I see it, and it's just another painful reminder of what was mine but now is not. The only thing that remains now is the minivan.

So now I am stuck with this minivan, which I do appreciate, but it's also the only vehicle parked in my driveway. Since I work Friday and Saturday night, I was a bit concerned with someone breaking into my home. My neighbor's house was hit during the day, and I felt an immediate need to do the next best thing- get a mean looking dog.

I had a dog. It's my daughter's, but nothing about the dog screams, *Don't you dare come into my yard or I'm going to bite your face off!* Four trips to the pound later and I found my dog. Her name is Wednesday. It was March Madness, so it was only $20 to adopt her. My dad had a gift card from 2001 that I gifted him for pet adoption. I had her microchipped, and the shelter honored the gift certificate. Out the door, she cost me $10. She's a pit bull, so she fits the bill when it comes to looking vicious. She's a sweetheart though. I named her Wednesday because I got her on Wednesday. My brain could not put that much thought into it.

Sam's Birthday

It's Sam's birthday, and our son has a game today. My son's performance has been affected by his father moving out of the house and all the drama that now surrounds Sam with this woman, Namah. I asked Sam not to bring her to the baseball games until after our divorce. All day I have been a wreck and often sneak off to my minivan to cry. Sam comments, "You should have stayed at home if you can't hold it together."

I have a feeling Namah is waiting in the parking lot for Sam after the game. My daughter and I are walking together out to my minivan. I try and call Sam on the phone to let him know we are leaving. I can see Sam in her vehicle. I yell for him. He hears me and steps out of her car. She then yells from across the parking lot, "Hi M!" in a snooty voice.

I flip her off and say, "Fuck you!" I am enraged that this woman is here at my son's game.

Sam says I should act more like a mother in front of my daughter. I asked him, "Why would she even speak to me? And why the

27

fuck is she here? She knows I don't like her. I made it very clear to you to keep her away from me."

Cut Off His Dick!

Now when I'm at the grocery store, or the gas station, or anywhere in public surrounded by other men; I think how much more vulnerable I am. Do they know by looking at me with my tired, red swollen eyes and the scorn look on my face that my husband has left me? And that every man I see I want to cut off his dick?!

Running from Himself

Steeped in denial, I knew what my heart was trying to tell me. The late nights or all-nighters, not answering my phone calls, the rants and raves when Sam did answer in his drunken state to blame me for everything that was wrong with our marriage. He wasn't running from me. He was running from himself.

Murdering My Reality

Do I dare ask him why he had his affairs? Ask for details? Do I want to rewrite the memories of us? All of it a lie!

I cannot bear the truth. All my memories from getting married, to having children, to imagining us old together will be replaced. That would be murdering my reality as I know it!

Vomit My Soul

He shared details of her. Bragged about her, how she makes more money than I ever will. How much better off my kids will be with her influence in their lives.

Can you believe that?! How can that woman be a good influence on my children?!

I wanted to vomit my soul out!

Four Words

Him: Will you marry me?
 I want a divorce.

Me: Fuck you mother fucker!

Dart Board

The pictures of Sam are everywhere. I leave them up for the kids. His face haunts me. He is alive but feels dead. His smile reminds me of the hopes and dreams we had together. I dare not touch them even though I would like to make a collage with them, hang it above my bed, and throw darts at it.

Social Status: Unknown

I must get used to the idea of being single again. This will take some time. I can already feel the vultures circling me. How do men know this shit? Or am I just now aware of this encroachment that's always been present by the opposite sex?

I threw all my old makeup away. I only wore it when Sam took me out. He rarely did; hence I had the same eyeshadow, lip gloss, blush, and face powder for years.

I don't want to think about dating. I hate men! I know this feeling will pass. Until then my Facebook status will be unknown.

The Counselor, Good Grief!

So now I'm expected to unload my shit to a stranger. And this is supposed to help me release my grief and anger? Here I go again reliving my life with Sam. I've been doing that a lot lately in my head. The memories of us seem so surreal; like they aren't even mine but someone else's life I saw in a movie.

There were happy times -most of them before we got married and had kids. Was that where we went wrong? He wanted kids so badly. He knew I did not. He even sent me away so that I could think about it. I stayed with my brother for a week. I went back to Sam and said that I wasn't going to let my fears of my upbringing prevent me from bringing children into this world. I knew I could offer a child a lot of love. That was a pivotal point in our relationship. There was no turning back. Marriage was the next step.

Not only am I sharing my history with Sam with my counselor, but also my dreams of Adam, the Invisible Lover. She asked me at the last session, "What M would you want from Adam if you did find out he feels the same about you?"

I give her a fake answer because my heart wants what I know it can never have, so I don't let my mind even go there.

Rise Above It

I can hear Sam's voice in my head, "For someone who's done yoga for twenty years and talks about God all the time, you sure aren't practicing what you've been preaching."

Am I supposed to act saintly? No one knows how they're going to act during a divorce. It's a traumatic, ugly, and ungodly experience. I want to throw the book, *The Four Agreements,* out the window of my minivan next time I am driving down the freeway and say to the universe FUCK YOU!

My therapist says it takes three times as long to move past a traumatic event. I told her it would take me less time. I estimated it based on how long it will take me to finish this book and publish it. Until then Fuck Everything!

Shedding Innocence

 With Sam gone, I see my kids- I mean really see them. I see that my daughter's insecurities have multiplied. My son's vulnerabilities have been unmasked. They are shedding their innocence right before my eyes. My daughter's fragile state of mind mirrors mine. My son's anger that is bottled up inside of him sometimes finds a way out.

 One morning before school he was putting on his belt. I was barking orders like a drill sergeant, "Hurry up- go, go, go, go, go!"

 Out of the blue, he says, "I hate dad!"

 I feel the anger and sadness in his voice. I walk over to him and say, "It's okay to be angry with him. You can't hate someone unless you love them first."

 It was at that moment I realized I need to be more patient, more attentive with my kids. Who cares if we're late for school? Sam leaving us meant to my son that it felt like the end of his world and I needed to ease up. Teeth will still get brushed, homework done, and kids will make it to school. Life will move on.

Ungodly

I wonder if people expect me to be composed, all godly, during this most ungodly time. Don't they know I am human? A woman whose heart has been ripped out of her chest? I feel betrayed. I also secretly want revenge.

Don't Date Me

I always wear skinny jeans, a wife beater tank, and Converse shoes. This is my signature wear. It says, 'Stay the fuck away from me! I'm unapproachable and not interested! If you look at me the wrong way, I will give you the stink eye. If you talk to me, my eyes will roll in the back of my head. I don't want to be looked at like a piece of meat. Lasers will shoot out of my eyes, and you'll be dead! I won't have any remorse for killing you. You're just another dick to me.'

I should just wear a warning label that reads: **Bitter Bitch! Stay Back!**

Wilted Flowers

He pretended to care. He bought me flowers for our last anniversary before he left me. Looking back, there was no letter, no card that expressed his love for me. They are just flowers that wilted away.

I can't remember the last time Sam expressed his love for me in that fashion. In the beginning, there were poems, cards, little notes left for me on my pillow — all of that dead. I guess his love for me died some time ago.

Reflection

Now when I look in the mirror, I don't see a completely helpless woman who was dependent on her husband financially, emotionally.

Instead, I see a warrior emerging from a battlefield- ready to face all the injustices in her life. And she demands restitution!

A Donkey

Oh, he blames me for loving an invisible lover. I tried to explain the nature of the Beloved* to him. His intellect could not grasp it. Seeing as he could not rise to meet me on my level, nor could I sink to his- I gave up.

Most men are led by the donkey of intellect. They work so hard to feed it and care for it. Jesus rode into Jerusalem on a donkey, and he dismounted the ass; leaving it behind.

Warning: Don't let your lusts guide you!

*Beloved is a common Sufi name for God as the object of love and spiritual desire. Can also be used to denote a human being who mirrors divine attributes.

My Battlefield

My battlefield has become my bedroom where I pick up the pen and paper to release my rage.

When I leave my house, which my daily duties force me to do, my battlefield is my car. There I blast as loud as my ears can stand it: Korn, Pantera, Mega Death, Ozzy, or Metallica- anything that gets this anger out of me and allows me to get through another day.

A Damn Train Wreck

Now, what do my family and friends expect from me? I am a destitute woman left in ruins. I was a partner to someone for almost twenty years. Now I'm expected to pull myself together and rise above my failing marriage, and pretend all is well?

I'm not an actress trained in the art of performing. This is my life! Society puts to much pressure on women to be well put together and to look good.

I'm a damn train wreck! And I won't pretend to be anything else than what I am right now.

Ring Finger

It's been almost four months since Sam left me. I still wear my wedding band. I'm scared to take it off. Scared it will make me feel naked- vulnerable. I don't want to be prey to godless men.

Sam hasn't worn his for years. His excuse was he works with his hands. But I know the real reason.

Answer

I do believe there was a time when Sam did love me. I was like his captive held hostage in his castle but didn't mind. I was the princess in need of being rescued by the handsome prince. I was an exotic dancer with no life skills or college education when he first met me.

With no job and no car, I was stranded at home a lot at the beginning of our relationship and well after our first child was born. I liked being at home and did not complain. I also loved being a stay at home mom and saw this as the most important job in the world.

I thought once Sam and I married things would be different. I thought Sam would be home more. I thought we'd sit down as a family for dinner more often than on holidays or special occasions, like when company was over. I thought we would find a good Christian church to attend on Sundays and our children would go to Sunday school.

Sure, there was happy, quality times spent together. The numerous Halloweens with matching costumes, the many family functions we attended hosted by my mother and father-in-law, vacations to the beach, and many more countless, beautiful memories I will have forever.

Looking back now, as a soon to be divorced 42-year-old woman, I feel I was more like his servant, maid, child bearer, nanny- nothing that gives me the feeling of being an equal partner.

Who taught me this? Where did I learn this role as a woman? As a wife? I'm going to have to investigate more into my subconscious to find a satisfying answer.

My Version of It

As I string together the last, almost twenty years of my life with Sam; who became my roommate, then my friend, then my lover, then my husband, and now my worst enemy, I sit here and wonder what his version of it is.

Paper Bag

I've done absolutely what I love- writing. And it's absolutely made me no money (which Sam reminded me often of). But I can't give it up. It would feel like breathing with a paper bag over my head!

Eating Words

In the first two weeks, 8 pounds seemed to slide off me like butter. I couldn't eat. My stomach was in knots. The smell of food made me nauseous. I still haven't digested Sam's words, "I'm Leaving. I Want A Divorce."

They were stuck in my throat. I tried to choke them down, but my heart would not allow it.

Lost and Found

   She's not entitled to my life! I have spent almost twenty years building my life with Sam- our friends, places we go, my children, all our possessions! And she gets to swoop right in and claim it! As if these are items in lost and found?! I won't have it!

Mouse Trap

Marriage is a trap! How come no one told me this? I was like a little mouse lured by the promise of cheese, only to be met by certain death.

Sam put me in his house and his bed with the promise of security and love. He failed to mention it came with a price. Don't question his late nights out and his suspicious phone calls.

I was supposed to act as a mouse and be content with the cheese he gave me?!

The Wrong Prayer

From a distance, our marriage looked good. I'm sure to our friends we appeared as the ideal couple. I grounded in my spirituality, offset Sam's less desirable traits.

I thought if I prayed hard enough God would change my husband into a virtuous man. I realize now I was praying the wrong prayer.

Sam's Haunting Voice

Sam's voice in my head narrates my life and my faults in our failing marriage. It says, "You should have gone to college made something of your life. You should have worked for a company that offered health insurance with benefits. You spend too much time doing unproductive stuff like reading, writing, and yoga. All that time you wasted on nonsense. None of it has made you any money. Your kids wear rags! Your daughter has holes in her pants. Your son's shirts are too small for him."

I would reply, "Well now you have a Sugar Momma to buy you and our children new clothes, shoes, whatever they need. I know how important all that stuff is to you. I certainly can't afford to buy my son underwear for $10 a pair! Nor can I afford to take my daughter to get pedicures. So, enjoy your new plastic life! You and Namah deserve each other! I'd rather die poor and with my integrity. Thank You Very Much!"

Flattery Does Help

On my birthday of all days, I filed my response to Sam's divorce petition. I felt like a felon convicted of a crime that I didn't commit as I walked into the courthouse. I was pleasantly greeted by a cop who asked me why I was there. I answered him and said, "To file my divorce papers."

He then asked," Are you the Petitioner or the Responder?"

I answered and said," The Responder."

He responded with, "He's a fool. You are beautiful! I am really sorry to hear that. One day you will find happiness."

I returned his flattery with a smile and said, "Thank you. I hope I do."

He probably says that to all the teary-eyed, heartbroken women that walk through his door. It didn't matter. What he said made me feel desirable again. It made the process of filing my papers easier that day and lifted my spirits.

My attitude towards men is changing. I no longer want to cut off all their dicks.

New State of Emergency

Once you enter the divorce world, there's this constant state of an emergency happening to you and all around you. I first noticed this to be true when my minivan wouldn't start. I was leaving gymnastics with my daughter, and the damn thing wouldn't turn over. I knew something was wrong because the problem began two days before. Five times I tried to start it.

On the sixth try, she started right up. I said, "Thank you, God!" I was able to start the minivan the next morning and take the kids to school. My dad came over after I told him the emergency I had. He checked the battery, and it was okay. In my gut, I knew I needed to take it to the dealership. My dad made sure I drove off with no problems before he left. I went straight to the dealership. I then asked God that the repairs wouldn't cost me more than what I had saved up for things like this.

For the past five months, I had been taking care of my husband's great aunt. On Thursdays, I'd go clean her house, do her laundry, and run any errands she needed me to do. She paid me $20 an hour. It usually took me two hours to do everything. I had saved up $540 since I started. The repairs were $480. I was just relieved I had enough money, and they were done in twenty-four hours.

It feels like one thing after another has been happening that keeps me on my toes and in a new state of unease. The one good paying client that I had been taking care of for the past six months left to her summer home in Northern California. Now it's a daily habit of mine to search Craigslist and jobing.com for CNA jobs. I need to find an employer that is flexible with the hours that I need to take my kids to school and pick them up. I hope to find something soon.

My Imaginary Suicide Note

My suicide note would read something like this:

To Family and Friends,

I am pretty confident by now that there is a better place than this hell hole. I don't want to be here. There is so much suffering in and around me. I'm 99.9% sure that God doesn't want me to suffer anymore. And, 99.9% sure that I am more valuable dead than alive. Maybe then my writing will take off. Maybe my sad fate is likened to Emily Dickenson or Thomas Paine.

To everyone who knew me, I can honestly say you did not know me. Make sure you have my body burned. I want my soul released from my body at once!

Hasta La Vista! Peace Out!

M

I'm Not A Wife Anymore, So Who Am I?

For nineteen years I was the other half of Sam. That is almost half of my life. He no longer wants me as his wife. I begin to wonder will anyone want me again.

Sam rejected me. I'm not a toy you can unwrap on Christmas that you love in the beginning, play with a lot at first, grow attached to, and then decide that you don't want it anymore because it's old, worn out, and not as shiny.

My daughter has a teddy bear that she got when she was a toddler. She cries when she can't find Teddy at bedtime. I end up looking for Teddy everywhere because I know it's the end of her world as she knows it.

One day she came home from school to discover Teddy was missing one of his eyes. Our family dog had chewed on Teddy like a bone. That didn't matter to her. She still picked Teddy up, squeezed him tightly, and showered him with kisses.

My grief counselor tells me, "M you need to bury the wife when you're ready."

I know she is right. Maybe I need to start thinking about her funeral service. I wonder if Sam would come.

Sam's Moral Compass

I can't help but think if Al, our neighbor, and Sam's dear friend were still alive, along with Sam's grandmother and mom that this would not be happening. They were Sam's moral compass.

Al would have given Sam a lecture about the value of family and would have said something like, "You stay in marriage through thick and thin."

Sam's mom would have said, "You're an idiot son!" Often this woman praised me on how good I took care of her son and repeatedly thanked me for it. God, I miss that lady!

His grandmother would have said," What the hell is wrong with you Sam? M is a good woman, a good wife, a good mother."

I miss them all very much. They are not here to be my soldiers though. This makes me believe that God has other plans for my life and being married to Sam is no longer one of them.

Food Boxes

Every weekend I pick up a food box from my dad. He started giving me the boxes knowing that I always have a house full of kids that are always hungry. There are a lot of kids on my street. On average there are 4-6 kids coming and going daily. I like being surrounded by kids especially during this emotionally hard time.

Often, I leave fruit out on the counter for them to eat. The kids know that anything left out is a *Free For All.* Sometimes I have too much food for my refrigerator and share it with my neighbors.

But now with Sam gone, I've come to rely on the food boxes. It is humbling and reminds me to give gratitude for having food. Not everyone in this world has food to eat.

Gee, how we could feed every human being if we stopped funding war machines. This fucking world is so spiritually sick!

The Poor House

Divorce will put you in the poor house.
When Sam left, I had to take the first job I
applied for just to make ends meet. It
happened to be a weekend third shift
position at a group home. The only good
thing was that it was a mile up the road from
where I live. The pay was not great, but the
owner and the staff were wonderful. I was
very grateful even to have a job at all. This
meant my ship wouldn't sink completely yet.

Sam was still paying the mortgage. But
now I was responsible for all the other bills.
There were doctor bills, utilities, phone,
groceries, gas for my vehicle and
maintenance. I became a squirrel saving up
bits of money for emergencies. I knew soon
I would have to take over the mortgage
payment and I would be responsible for my
health and auto insurance.

I planned to get a better paying job that
supported my lifestyle. I also needed to start
building my credit and apply for a credit
card. If I had a plan in place and followed
through, then this all wasn't so
overwhelming and even seemed possible to
do on my own. I didn't care if I didn't have

money to splurge on things like shoes or movie tickets. I just wanted to provide a loving home for my kids and prove to them and everyone that I can do this on my own. I don't need a man in my life.

My Inner Sparkle

My daughter exclaims, "Now you're shimmerized!" After she and her best friend paint my nails a bold purple with a bright pink accent color. The girls give me a foot massage, back rub, and braided my hair back like the princess in the movie Princess Bride.

She tells me I need to get more in touch with my inner girl- how I wear too much black and grey, and how I'm too much of a Tomboy. Where does she come up with this stuff? I have to agree with her. I need to put on a sparkling party dress and five-inch heels that shimmer with a dazzling eyeshadow and a red lipstick that says, "Look out world! Ready or not here I come!"

Please, May I Reserve My Children?

So far, Sam has been taking the kids on the weekends. He picks them up at 3 pm on Fridays and returns them at 8 pm on Sundays. Mother's Day is approaching, and we haven't had our day in court yet, which will decide the parenting time.

So, like an intended patron of a restaurant, calling to reserve my table for the evening, I put in my reservation and politely request, "Please may I have the kids on Mother's Day?"

In my head I imagined the phone conversation would go something like this:

Me: I hope it's not too much to fucking ask, but I thought that fucking maybe I could have my children on Mother's Day? After all, I did birth them and am raising them even after you left us for Namah. So, may I please have my children on that Sunday you piece of shit!?"

Him: I would never deny you having the kids on Mother's Day. And yes, I know I'm a piece of shit.

Me: Thanks, please pencil me in for ALL DAY May 17.

Oh brother, is this what it all comes down too? My new normal?

Giving Birth to a Corpse

As I sit here, and the realization hits me that my marriage to Sam is over, I am pregnant with a corpse. Soon I will have to give birth to it. I don't feel any labor pains yet, but I would calculate that I am at the beginning of my second trimester. I am miserable and feel helpless.

I must make sure that I don't feed my depression and put on weight. God, I just want this pregnancy to be over. This could also be the death of me.

My Letter to Invisible Lover

Dear Invisible Lover,

Since I have come clean with my husband about our invisible love affair, my life is now in shambles. My husband, along with most of my friends and family, now know of your existence (or to be more accurately put) your nonexistence. Some think I should be locked up, institutionalized. Some think I am just pitiful and therefore should be pitied. And then there are a few that hope (for my sake) that you are real. Like me, they want to believe in everlasting, divine love.

My grief counselor thinks I am only grieving the loss of my husband. But deep down I also am grieving the loss of you. I know I cannot continue with this fantasy.

Please know that it was my choice to risk it all and, in the end, it may cost me all. And even though my feelings for you may be real, I must let go of the notion of you actually materializing before my eyes.

I want to say thank you for all your invisible support over the years. How oddly real it has all felt to me. Secretly, I will always wish you are real and that you are the knight in shining armor that I've been dreaming about all these years.

Wherever you are- whether in the ether, in my thoughts, in my heart, in my dreams, or light years away- I will always be grateful for the unconditional love that floods my soul every day. May God have mercy on me that I meet you on the shores of Eternity and be lost into your eyes again.

Love Me Always

Three Words

Eat shit asshole! I feel betrayed. I feel alone. I feel beaten. I feel enslaved. I feel superficial. I feel small. I feel regret. I feel mistreated. I feel remorse. I feel confused. I feel deceived.

You lied asshole! You cheated repeatedly. I am numb. I am angry. I am bitter. I am ungodly. I am dead. I am complicated.

You are hopeless. You're a demon. You're a monster. You are cold. You are insensitive. You are foolish. You are ignorant. You are deranged. You are uncaring. You are unkind. You are unloving. You are unworthy. You are dead! You are shameful. You are despised. You are reckless.

Remember our lives? Remember my pain? Remember my sacrifices? Remember my burdens? Remember your neglect? Remember our love? Remember our family? Remember our friends? Remember our work? Remember our joy? Remember our laughter? Remember our pain? Remember my heart? Remember my face? Remember my body?

You forgot me. You lost me. You abandoned me. You forsaken me. You confuse me. You despise me. You reject me. You imprison me.

I am free. I am untangled. I am done! I am unattached. I am unloved. I am unwanted. I am numb. I am depressed. I am gone.

Eraser Man

My dad stopped by this morning to bring me a food box. It happened to be the day after Mother's Day. This is the first Mother's Day I spent without my kids. I had to start my new job with better hours and pay, which I am grateful for and now I can quit working the night shift. So, my kids got to spend it with Sam and Namah. I spent Saturday crying all day. I know I have to adjust to my new life, but not spending Mother's Day with the children I birthed into this world sickens my soul.

My dad gives his wise fatherly advice and says, "M you have to be patient with yourself and adjust to your new circumstances."

I agree. He then goes on to say, "The years with Sam must feel like they just have been erased."

I think to myself how this is true and acknowledge that my soul feels like a blank chalkboard. It was full of Sam. All our living that we did together is now erased- now VOID.

Eraser Man in my head comments, "This wasn't made to last forever. Your life with Sam is now a fading dream and needs to be buried in the past."

Eraser Man makes me painfully realize a simple truth that I already know, but now has become my living truth- everything does get erased and fades away with time. I'm just not ready to let Sam go.

The Two Armies

Once your friends get word of your divorce, then they become like two armies on the battlefield. The friends that are true to you form behind your line. These friends have your back. They are there to give you ammo when you need it. I've gotten advice on the legal stuff, parenting matters, and dating (when that happens).

Then there are the friends who were both you and your husband's. They disappeared. At least for now. I mostly do not hear from them. In my mind, they have taken Sam's side. I'm sure he's convinced them all how crazy I am (the God loving freak that I am). Or they just don't want to get involved. I actually can't blame them. But they are now Sam's army since Sam keeps in touch with them and I do not.

Then there are the deserters who abandon you completely. They avoid you like the plague. These friends, I realize, we're never a friend to begin with. So, you just write them off, and when you do run into them, you just smile a big fake smile. Underneath you're a hot mess, but you don't let them see.

Today I fucking hate you

Dear Ahole,

This morning your daughter had a meltdown. Maybe her ear was bothering her. Maybe it was me rushing her to hurry and get ready for school. I tried to call you thinking you could talk to her and ease her, but like always you didn't answer your phone. Now I just want to say I fucking hate you!

Then as we made it to school, she is no longer crying. I am relieved, but now I want to cry. I should be able to handle all of this. Shit, I've been doing all of it all these years anyway. You were always gone, or if you were home, you were occupied on your phone and reminded me not to bother you. You'd say, "This is a business call. One of us has to pay the bills."

As your remarks echo in my mind, I become enraged, and I fucking hate you. While you were on the phone, I was raising our kids: helping them with their homework, wiping their tears, taking them to school and picking them up, taking them to their play dates; your daughter to her dance, gymnastics, choir, swim, and art classes. I also was shopping for household supplies, making the meals, budging the family budget, budgeting your business (expense reports, estimates, invoices, collections), unclogging toilets, changing light bulbs, taking out the trash, doing all the landscaping, housekeeping, laundry, going to birthday parties.

I'm sure there are things I have forgotten here. And all of that runs through my mind. And I think how you can't pick up the fucking phone when your kids need you!? Go fuck yourself!

Later, in the day, your son has a meltdown. Yes, he's thirteen and should be able to process his emotions better than his sister. This time homework is the trigger. He spent 30 minutes on a timeline and had to start it all over. In error, he was doing it for the wrong war. He says how he hates himself and wishes he was dead. Now for the third time in one day, I think to myself how much I fucking hate you! I hug him and tell him to go play that I will help him later. I know he needs his dad. And I know it's killing him that you're playing daddy to another kid his age.

P.S- Time will eventually heal our hearts. We will get use to you being gone. Until then you might want to pick up the fucking phone, so your kids know you still do care and they are your priority. And maybe reassure them that you do love them. But we will be fine for I'm not going anywhere. I am their rock. And I will always make them my priority and reassure them they are loved and there is nothing to fear- for Mommy has God as her rock and one day He will be theirs too.

The Mother of Your Children

Singles Ad

While Sam is off on Fantasy Island with Namah, I'm pretty sure I've killed my chance of finding true happiness. It's a lot easier to go through life half asleep. I'm not one of them. Sam was threatened by my spiritual gifts. And I refuse to live my life as a *closet mystic*. God help the man that's brave enough to date me! My singles ad would read something like this:

I have twenty years of experience with dream yoga, astral projection, tonglen meditation, demonology, out of body experiences, lucid dreaming. My other abilities include telepathy, empathic, remote viewing, automatic writing, and channeling.

I'm pretty sure this is enough to scare any guy away.

Shade of Black

My memories are jumbled of Sam and me. They are like one long stretch of freeway that you've been driving on for hours and the lines begin to blur. The memories seem unreal, like none of it happened- yet they did. All my memories now are buried in the past. To put them and Sam in their final resting place, I need to have a funeral. I always did look good in any shade of black.

Romantic Eulogy

Sam and M met when they were in their twenties; M was 23 and Sam was 27. Their circumstances were a bit unusual. Sam was M's roommate. Soon there was a friendship that blossomed between them. They were inseparable in the beginning- fused at each other's side. They adored each other and in time became best friends.

Sam's proposal to M was not unexpected. M without hesitation said yes. They married on New Year's Eve, 2002, in honor of Sam's grandparents' wedding anniversary. Their picture-perfect marriage lasted over sixty years.

Sam and M had a near brush with death on Easter weekend returning from their honeymoon in Vegas. Their vehicle rolled five times on the freeway. A year later, their first child was born. M gave birth to the son Sam always wanted.

Not long after that, their marriage survived another blow. Sam's string of infidelities almost destroyed them. Sam soon after making a new commitment to M. He vowed to be a better husband.

With a fresh new start, M became pregnant with their second child in 2007, a little girl that she always wanted. Things were looking up. Little Sam followed in his dad's footsteps and played baseball. Sam put his heart and soul into his son. M put her energy into raising their children.

Looking from the outside in, they were an admired couple with two beautiful kids. That's why it is so sad, so heartbreaking to see the death of this power couple Sam and M. They inspired their friends and were a light to others. They will be sorely missed together at family gatherings, friends' parties, and social functions. May they both find everlasting peace. They are survived by their son and daughter.

What I treasured, Foot Salad!

Sam had a great sense of humor. Every day he made me laugh. I will miss that. One story we'd often bring up repeatedly is the story of the foot salad. No matter how many times I have heard Sam tell it, it made me laugh every time.

We had our dear friends over for dinner. I made a salad with green leaf lettuce, shredded carrots, English cucumbers, feta cheese, croutons, avocados, and red onions. We had pasta as the main course with garlic bread and red wine.

I had a small round table that seated four. The table was elegantly set, and the food served. Sam had been helpful and placed the salad I had made in a ceramic bowl that was a wedding gift. When I saw the bowl, I was horrified! Immediately I pulled Sam aside and said, "By the way, that is the bowl I use to soak your feet in, and I never wash it. I only use it for your feet."

He replied, "That's okay. We just won't tell them. It doesn't bother me; it's my feet after all."

We never told our friends about the foot salad. It was our little secret over the years. I remember the husband commenting, "This is very good!"

Dinner by Candle Light, What's That?

I used to enjoy cooking for Sam. I'd try out new recipes. We'd have guests over, and I would look forward to Chicken Cor Don Blu, lasagna from scratch, or lobster and shrimp scampi.

It made me happy to feed Sam's appetite, and I always wanted his opinion on my kitchen experiments. That phase ended when we had children. No more dinner planning. What took two hours in the kitchen, needed to be done in less than thirty minutes. Good luck finding a meal that everyone likes. And when you did it permanently stays on the weekly menu.

Sam got tired of this real quick. Not only that but the many other little disturbances that come along with two kids. No more dinners by candlelight. Candles were now a fire hazard. Our time spent sharing our day ended abruptly when Sam no longer joined us for dinner.

He was always working, and if he was home, he was always on the phone working. There was no time to sit down as a family and share our day. And that wasn't how I was brought up. Dinners together didn't seem like a priority to Sam anymore. Maybe I didn't want to admit it then, but it was beginning to slowly chip away my marriage.

Now Sam seemed to complain all the time. He'd say, "The food is undercooked. The food is overcooked. Where's the beer? Why isn't there a cold mug in the freezer? Why are the dishes still dirty if you washed them in the dishwasher? Did the kids have a vegetable with their dinner? If the kids don't like what you make them, make them something they do like. I want my kids to eat!"

Sam had turned into a kitchen Nazi.

Expiration Date

My marriage is Done. Over. Finished. If it were a carton of milk it would read: **Good until sex is nonexistent, sexual appetite diminished, candlelight dinners a thing of the past, lingerie night substituted for pajama night and Disney movies, shower for two changes it's meaning to shower for mommy and daughter or daddy and son, naked time is now a three-year-old running around protesting clothes, sex is now a duty or when can I pencil you in.**

This is how you know you've reached your expiration date. With Sam, we hit that expiration date after our son was born. Sam's needs were now on the back burner, and this little package of poop, screams, and giggles demanded me first. I had to make sacrifices, which also meant my needs were no longer being met.

I love being a mom. I recognized the sacrifices I needed to make. I embraced the new season of motherhood. I tried to balance my mommy duties with my wifely duties. I can honestly say that I did my best to try and make Sam happy. At the end of the day, only Sam can make Sam happy.

Pass the Knife Please

My one friend, that was so kind to call me to inform me that she saw Sam at Hooters with another woman; her husband now hosts pool parties and invites Sam, Namah, and my children. Sam has forced Namah down his families and friends' throats where they are demanded to chew, swallow, and digest his relationship with Namah.

I just sit at home and hear the random gossip or see things posted on Facebook. I read the comments, which is very unhealthy for my emotional wellbeing and why I torture myself in this fashion, I do not know. I notice the friends that I thought were my friends, liking the photos and I feel betrayed and disrespected by them. I find it all revolting.

I want to scream, "Someone pass the knife, please! There's a line of random friends that have joined Sam's camp and wish to stab his soon to be ex-wife in the back!"

Someone Call an Attorney!

Count it all joy, my brethren, when you meet various trials, for you know that the testing of your faith produces steadfastness. James 1:2

Today I came home from work and found a letter in my mailbox from an attorney. We've already been to our first resolution conference and divided our assets. The only thing that was left unresolved was the parenting time and child support.

That day in court I thought went well. Sam and I agreed that I could stay in the house to raise our kids. That night Sam called. It was Monday, and he still had the kids. I was to meet him to pick them up. When I answered the phone, he screamed at me, "You are not getting the kids! I am filing for emergency custody! You are crazy! Namah is filing a restraining order on you for when you attacked her in January!"

I had no idea where all this anger was coming from all of a sudden. Then the threatening text messages started about how I need to move out of the house and berating me as a mother. I ignored the messages.

There was a court order in place from our first resolution conference. It stated that Sam and I would be Tenants in Common regarding our home. I found out through my husband's email, that I still had access to, that Namah and Sam were hiring an attorney to try and reverse the court order because she wanted my house sold. She wanted to buy a bigger house, and this tied up any plans she had to get a new home loan with Sam. There were also emails from a realtor with houses for sale they were looking at.

Sam later confirmed that Namah paid the attorney's retainer fee. I had no choice, I had to get an attorney. The only title I had in my name was for a 2002 Toyhauler. I placed an ad on Craigslist and sold it for $6500. Half of it went to the attorney I hired, Faith. The other half went into my savings.

Kung Fu Panda

I fantasize about being ten years old again. I would tell Namah to meet me on the playground after school so that I can kick her ass!

"Oh yeah bitch, you want to post pictures on FB of my kids with my husband as a *Happy Family* when I'm not even divorced yet?"

I would do my kung fu panda on her face first. Then I would sidekick her in the torso Bruce Lee style. Lastly, when she falls to the ground, I would do my Hulk Hogan body slam right on top of her.

I'm sure she would tap out.

The Shittiness

This is Shitty! There are no other words to put to this. My husband is gone- Shitty! He's with another woman- Shitty! I feel like a failure, a loser- Shitty! Bills are piling up- Shitty! I have to explain to the kids why mommy and daddy are getting a divorce- Shitty! Holidays are now split with soon to be ex-husband and without the in-laws- Shitty! This feeling that I will never trust another man again- Shitty!

The Longmire Way

I had to file an Order of Protection against Sam. It was a Monday night, and my phone rang. I answered when I saw that it was Sam. He screamed, "You ruined my life!"

I had been receiving harassing text messages from Sam's phone. I had been ignoring them and wanted to block his number. I couldn't though because that is how I communicated with him about our kids.

So, you could say that in the back of my mind I had a feeling that Sam was going to say or do something and take it to a whole new level. There were two separate phone calls he made that night. The first he ranted and raved about how crazy I am. He told me I have thirty days to move out of my house and that he's moving back in to raise the kids.

In the middle of the craziness, I was watching Longmire. Longmire was investigating a murder. I had the presence of mind to grab my hand-held cassette recorder and record Sam. I only recorded a portion of the first phone call. Sam was dumb enough to call back thirty minutes later. That phone call I recorded the whole thing. He sounded like a demon screaming at me through the phone. He cursed, "I am going to kill you and bury you!"

I was shaking so bad after I hung up. I paced back and forth in my home. I could not sit. The air around me felt heavy. Each breath I took was painful. I collected myself and emailed my attorney right away. I wrote, "I need to see you in the morning. My husband just called and threatened to kill me! I recorded it. Please call me right away."

She emailed me right back to tell me she had to be in court in the morning. I went ahead and voiced recorded the threats to my phone so that I could email them to her.

First thing in the morning she called me and said, "M you need to go file an Order of Protection against Sam. He doesn't just say it once he wants to kill you, but five times."

So, when I got off work Tuesday, I went straight to the courthouse and filed my Order of Protection. I instantly felt the space in my chest expand. I could breathe again.

Bitch What? An Assault Charge!

In retaliation of my Order of Protection on Sam, the next day Namah filed a police report from the incident back in January. That was the night she drove my minivan home with my husband and son.

A detective called me to ask me about the assault. I told him everything from the affair my husband was having with Namah to how they both lied about it when I confronted them. I explained how I was completely blindsided that night. I remarked, "I did not expect to see this woman in my minivan!"

The detective said, "Unfortunately you are between a rock and a hard place. This will have to be reviewed by the city prosecutor's office. They will decide whether or not to press charges. If you don't get anything in the mail from them, that's probably a good sign."

All I could think was, *Wow what a bitch! Namah is woman enough to have an affair with my husband, but not woman enough to handle some hair pulling!?*

She told the detective she lost an earring that night. He asked me if I remembered seeing an earring. His question sent me into a fury. All I could think was that my marriage is over and all she's worried about is an earring?! I calmly replied to the detective, "No I don't remember an earring."

Third Party Interference

For months now, I was still being harassed by crazy text messages. The messages were long, which isn't Sam's style. He is short and to the point. My friends and family told me just to ignore the texts. That is easier said than done. They didn't know what it was like to be going through a bad divorce, and on top of it, the crazy ass girlfriend is making your life a living hell too. My attorney's remark on the text messages after she read them was, "Unfortunately third parties will get involved and interfere with a couple's divorce."

A week after I filed the Order of Protection in August (which allows me to contact Sam through text messaging or email only); I received two novel long text messages from Namah's phone. This confirmed my suspicion that she had been texting through Sam the whole time. In her messages, she tells me to no longer text Sam, that I need to text through her now. She brings up the attack on her with several exaggerations, gives me mothering advice, and parenting time solutions for my kids, and on and on and on.

I block her number and smudge my sacred space with sage. I don't want her negative energy lingering in the air around me. I think to myself, *Gee this is who my kids go to and spend their time with on the weekends, Lord Help Me!*

EBT Baby

For anyone who does not know what an EBT card is, it is a card issued by the Department of Security that allows you to buy food and get cash (if you also qualified for cash benefits).

I felt I didn't have a choice. My husband stopped the voluntary child support payments. He refused to give any more financial support towards his kids until there was a court order in place. I had no idea how much longer this would drag out through the courts with lawyers now involved.

It was the end of summer, and my lawyer said there might be no resolution until next year. I was on a sinking ship. My job was paying enough to pay all the bills, but that was it.

I felt like that impoverished child again. Flashbacks of my mom on welfare flooded my head. I remember how embarrassing it was to go to the store with her. Back then, the state issued booklets of money especially distinguished for food, called Food Stamps. Everyone knew you were poor if you had the book.

The day the letter arrived in the mail, I was terrified. What if I didn't qualify? I opened the sealed envelope to read, **you have been approved**. Tears of joy ran down my face. I thanked God for another prayer He answered.

Side note: The state also approved me for ACHHHS (medical coverage).

Dodge Ball

There were five attempts made to serve Sam the Order of Protection. Here is the list of the attempts made by the officer:

1. No answer at the door.

2. No answer again. The officer calls the listed number. Sam answers and says he will call him back. He does not.

3. The officer spoke with a man. He told the officer Sam was not there but should be back any minute. The officer waited twenty minutes. He did not show up.

4. No answer and officer still hasn't received a call back from Sam.

5. No answer at the alternate address listed. The order is returned **unserved.**

Court 9/14- I arrive at the courthouse twenty minutes early. I speak to the deputy that greets me at the entrance. I tell him, "I need to serve my husband an Order of Protection."

He replies, "Wait over there, and I will have someone come out to talk to you."

A woman in uniform appeared and instructed me that after my hearing, I am to leave the courtroom first. She would then have the judge request that my husband is to remain in the courtroom to be served.

I never made eye contact with him during the hearing. He felt like a stranger to me. I cannot believe I was married to this man that I now fear. I had the taste of cigarette ashes stuck in my throat. I do not smoke; haven't in many years.

Someone Call in the Swat Team

I was feeling bad for myself and having a pity party. There was no one around to hear my cries.

Then I remembered my two dogs, my tortoise, my chickens, and cat. I went outside to be with them. I have a beautiful, lush, green yard with mature trees and oleanders that border the property. I often retreat to my yard to walk and clear my head.

As I began walking laps in my backyard, I noticed I was being followed. There they were- my Swat Team. They followed me around the yard. Their presence lifting my spirit.

Forty Winks

Since Sam has left my sleep has been restless. I wake up more tired than when I went to sleep. The surge of anxiety brought on by stress and the pressure of being a single mom responsible for two kids, two dogs, a cat (plus a stray cat), a tortoise, and two chickens seizes me in the middle of the night.

To better manage my days, I squeeze in a forty winks nap. Twenty to thirty minutes is sufficient enough for me to recharge my batteries. I usually listen to relaxing sleep music to help me fall asleep. Oh, and I shut my door and tell the kids not to disturb me (they usually barge in anyway).

If you are wondering, the phrase forty winks come from Dr. Kitchiner's 1821 self-help guide, *The Art of Invigorating and Prolonging Life*. In his book, he says, "A Forty Winks Nap, in a horizontal posture, is the best preparative for any extraordinary exertion of either body or mind."

Public Defender to the Rescue!

My attorney, Carol, was upbeat and a seasoned public defender. Right away I felt at ease, and my fears subsided. I was pulled into a conference room, and we spoke about the assault charge against me. I gave her all my evidence that I had to show that Namah's claim was an act of retaliation.

I filed my Order of Protection against my husband August 15. She filed a police report the following day for the assault that happened in January. But in her report, she claimed bodily injury, death threats I supposedly made, and a missing caret diamond earring that she was seeking restitution for.

Carol explained to me and said, "Unfortunately sometimes spouses use the criminal justice system as leverage with custody rights when going through the Family Court. The court system can be unjust, but you did admit to pulling her hair. You have no criminal record, so I will ask for a Dissolution if you agree to a plea of guilty and take Anger Management classes. She continued to say, "This I feel is the best option for you and it won't go on your record. Unfortunately, you will have to pay her for the value of the diamond earring she claims she lost if she has a receipt for it."

I responded angrily, "There was no diamond earring."

Carol responded with sympathy, "Regardless if she lied about it or not, it will be part of the plea agreement you take today. It's not worth it. You can put this behind you and move on with your life. It's just a small price to pay."

Tears filled my eyes. I was outraged and commented, "She destroys a relationship I had for almost twenty years and lies about a damn earring she loses, and I have to pay her!"

We headed back into the courtroom where I stood before the judge. I greeted her Honor with a smile as I stood at the pulpit in front of her bench. The judge asked Carol, "Who is the plaintiff in this case?"

She responded, "It's the defendant's husband's girlfriend."

I silently chuckled as she tried to slyly convey the nature of the incident to her Honor.

The judge corrected her and responded, "I mean her name."

I agreed to the Dissolution and signed the court documents. This was one of the hardest days in this whole divorce nightmare. My dad went with me for support. I would have to say that this is the one time in my life that I've needed him the most.

A Season of Yielding

What we cannot bear removes us from life; what remains can be borne. Marcus Aurelius

A cake of pain with layers and layers of grief, anger, and resentment is what I was living off of every day. I tried to compromise, bargain with myself. I told myself I would focus on my kids, my work, fixing up my house — anything to rid myself of the pain.

None of this was working. Deep down I knew it would take years to heal. There was no shortcut to the other side of divorce. I envisioned coming out the other side a stronger, confident woman who had claimed her independence. But to become that woman, I would have to nail myself to my pain and claim it.

The new mantra that I repeat in the mirror is from Christina Perri. The song is titled, I Believe. *This is not the end of me; this is the beginning. This is not the end of me; this is the beginning. This is not the end of me; this is the beginning.* I repeat this up to ten times if I feel the need.

Permanent Furniture

There's a feeling when you are going through a divorce that you are going to break into a million pieces. I didn't want to burden my friends, family, or my dad with my ongoing problems. It seemed that once one problem was solved, another one would land in my lap. I found myself asking God how much can a person take.

There were those days when I felt like I was drowning and upside down, and I found myself on many occasions having to ask someone for a life jacket. It was my pride that was getting in the way of not wanting to ask for help. I began to see this as an obstacle on my path. Instead, I opened myself up to those closest to me that loved me and wanted to be there for me. I was making myself more vulnerable in my immediate relationships. I wasn't just healing myself but healing apart of them too. Like my sister-in-law who said to me," For years I have longed to be closer to you M."

On the day I had to go to court for Namah's assault charge I was relieved and depressed. I remember walking through the door when I got home, sitting at my bar, and

113

suddenly, I got a text from my sister-in-law. She said, "Hey I just wanted to check in and see how you were doing?"

I replied, "I just got back from court. Is that why you texted me?"

She replied, "No, I forgot. We are like sisters, connected."

I confirmed her suspicion.

Both of my sisters-in-law have turned out to be more than just the title given through marriage, but a permanent fixture, like a piece of furniture that you know will stay with you until you die because it is so beautiful, unique, and fits your personality so well. Some of my relationships had fallen apart, but some were being improved and reshaped.

A Slow Change

The signature pain that comes with divorce
is best described as being swept up in a
tornado and then dropped into a volcano to
burn to death.

Often, I found myself crying in my
minivan. It's like I held it in all day until I
was done with work, running my errands, or
dropping my kids off at school. And then
uncontrollably I would weep. I kept my
sunglasses on so other drivers didn't see a
pathetic, broken, middle-aged woman losing
it. It felt like this ache inside my chest would
surely kill me if I didn't submit to it.

I knew I was healing, but this was torture!
I wondered if I would ever fully recover. I
slowly began to notice a change in myself. I
was calmer, more present with my kids-
listening to their concerns or things they
wanted to share about their day. I enjoyed
the cool air in the morning as the kids and I
headed out for the day.

With Sam gone my home had become
more peaceful. There was less drama, fewer
messes to clean up. I didn't worry about
laundry, dishes, house chores- those things

simply got done when I was good and ready. The faint demanding voice of Sam in the back of my head was beginning to fade. And I welcomed the change it brought.

Invisible

I've had time to reflect on my marriage with Sam. He and I did not communicate well. I asked myself why this was the case. I always skirted around important issues like finances, my feelings, and other concerns. With Sam, there was always the fear of being rejected or shut out by him completely. I learned, over the years, to wait for the right moment to bring up money matters or other problems. If it was in the morning, I made sure he had his cup of coffee and the first shit of the day. If it was in the evening, I made sure he had dinner and a beer first.

I now ask myself why did I put up with this lack of communication or this feeling like a bomb is going to explode if I wasn't diligent in my delivery and timing of my concerns. I should have felt safe in the confidence of also sharing my feelings with him.

The more I take a deeper look into my role as his wife; the more I realize how invisible I felt in my marriage. The most important issues were never talked about. Sadly, I kept those secrets bottled up tightly inside of me for years.

I became the bomb that exploded that night when I assaulted Namah. All those years of feeling like my thoughts, dreams, and feelings didn't matter suddenly came rushing to the surface- along with the betrayal and the disgust. It was the first time I lost control of myself completely. Looking back on that night, Namah is lucky she kept her seatbelt on.

The Woman I Am Becoming

Despite all the hell I've been through in the past nine months, I do stop and pause to think about the woman I am becoming. My dreams are shedding light on the parts of me that are transforming. They are revealing my inner struggles and the path I am currently on.

My dream of parachuting tells me I am fearless and to trust myself. In another dream, I drown four men in a flooded basement. This translates to putting an end to the powerless feelings and the dominating controlling influences that men have projected onto me in the past. I'm balancing the masculine energies out within me and taking control of these influences that are buried in my subconscious.

One of my favorite dreams was of me riding a bicycle on a dirt road. I was all alone, enjoying the scenery. I was doing good pedaling on my own volition.

I know the road I travel is a road I travel alone, but it's my road, and I'm getting to my destination on my own power. The road

119

being dirt implies it will take effort, time, and perseverance to reach my dreams.

Roadside Service with a Cup of Piss

My minivan breaks down two blocks from the kids' school. I look at my son and daughter calmly and say, "Looks like you're walking the rest of the way, but you better run, you only have two minutes before the first bell."

I am waiting for AAA and must pee really bad. I grab my insulated blue coffee cup and decide I can no longer hold it and I relieve myself. I am wearing a fall colored cotton skirt. I got it from Maggie's Place for a dollar. The thrift store proceeds go to a shelter for women of domestic abuse. I think to myself I am now labeled as one of those women by the court system because of my Order of Protection. But I refuse to see myself as a victim, walking around with a stamp on my forehead that reads either: **Battered Wife, Fragile Woman, Defected Divorcee**. Nope, not me. I will not allow what I am going through to define who I am.

Tom pulls up in his old beat up VW bug. I called him for a ride. I open the door, climb in carefully, there is crap everywhere. He helps me put on my seat belt. We drive off to my dad's, so I can borrow my mom Sue's

121

car. It is cold; the windows don't roll up. I comment," Good thing I'm wearing my sweat jacket."

Tom replies, "It's a beautiful day." I think to myself, yes, it is a beautiful day. The forty-minute drive to my dads' and all I smell is Tom's pipe. I hold my breath when he lights it and turn my head toward the window. Tom is a good guy. I've been friends with him for eight years. Our kids go to school together. I can call him last minute for shit like this.

We get to my dad's house, and my dad tells me he has to take my mom Sue to the hospital again. I can hear the worry in his voice. I've lost count how many times she's gone this year. I say nothing; I have no words of comfort.

I drive away wondering if I'm going to be flat broke this Christmas. Three days later my mechanic calls to tell me my minivan is ready. The total bill is $861.24. I drain my savings and checking account and charge the rest to my credit card. This sucks!

I ask Sam again for the title to my minivan. Four days later I get a reply, "There is no clear title." I know it's Namah responding to my text. I think to myself what a bitch! Now she's holding my title hostage?! God, I would love to pee in her morning coffee cup and see the look on her face when she takes a drink.

Divorce Care

And whenever you stand praying, forgive, if you have anything against any one; so that your Father also who is in heaven may forgive you your trespasses. Mark 11:25

I discovered Divorce Care one day when I was at a local church with a client of mine that likes to walk on the indoor track. As we are standing at the elevator, I see a flyer that says **Divorce Care** in bold letters. If you are not familiar with Divorce Care, it is a nationwide program that meets once a week for twelve weeks. They help you move through the painful stages of divorce. They offer a safe place to share your painful experience with others that are going through the same thing.

I benefited the most from the group by understanding that what I am feeling is quite normal and that I am not alone. I could openly share my wounds, and I got insights from others who have or are going through a divorce. It taught me to trust that God does have a plan for my life after divorce. So now the question I ask myself is, *How do I see my divorce? Is it a fresh start?*

One of the epiphany's that I had during one of the topics on *forgiveness* was that if God can forgive me for all my sins, then I too can forgive my husband for all the pain he has caused me. This I know will take time, perhaps years, but I am willing to forgive and let go.

Anger Management

I am sitting in a wooden chair. There are ten of us in a circle. There are two other women in the group. I notice the heavy, looming vibe right away. As I sit, my arms are crossed, blocking my solar plexus, I do not like the feeling. One woman stinks like she hasn't bathed in weeks. I notice the young Mexican guy with the gold rings on all his fingers and the gold chain around his neck.

And then, the counselor walks in, and she's not at all what I expected. She's a damn Barbie doll! She's tall, long blond hair, a perfect smile with polished white teeth, and at least ten years younger than me.

She greets the room, "Hello, I am Tiffany. If this is your first night, please introduce yourself. I see two new faces, so tell us your name and why you are here." She looks down at her roster and asks, "Who is M?"

I respond by raising my hand. I tell the group quite frankly, "I am part of the Positive Alternative Diversion Program. I am here because of an assault charge."

One guy from across the room jumps in and asks, "Who did you assault?"

I answer him with, "My husband's mistress."

The guy next to me replies, "You should get a free pass for that."

Tiffany reacts to his statement and says, "Responding with violence is never the answer. There are better ways to deal with anger." Tiffany then makes a list on the board of healthy outlets for feelings of anger: exercise, breathing, meditating, doing a hobby you love, writing, talking to a friend, etc.

I think to myself I'm already doing this. The one thing that helped me feel better was when I took Sam's favorite coffee mug; it read **Best Dad** and throwing it with all my might at his garage. From there on out I resorted to a football. It was the best therapy!

For the next ten weeks, Tiffany etches into our brains the words **DEAR MAN**: **D**escribe, **E**xpress, **A**ssert, **R**einforce, (stay) **M**indful, **A**ppear Confident, **N**egotiate.

And the use of "I" statements. "I feel _____ when you _____ because _____."

My I statement to Sam: I feel this technique is useless when you, Sam, don't even communicate with me because you're a damn coward.

My I statement to Namah: I feel pretty confident that the day will come when you will wish you could crawl back under the rock you came out from because you will feel shame.

Mental Status: Schizophrenic

It is the day of our Parenting Conference. Today we decide our children's parenting schedule. The kids have adapted to Sam picking them up from school on Fridays. He has been keeping them through the weekend and takes them to school on Mondays. I then pick them up from school on Monday and keep them until Friday morning, where I hug and kiss them goodbye as I drop them off at school.

Because of the OOP, Sam and I are interviewed separately. Two women evaluate our mental health and take notes throughout the meeting. We each discuss what we want for our parenting schedule and our concerns regarding the other parent.

I let Sam go first and sit in the lobby and read a book appropriately titled, *When Things Fall Apart*, while I wait for my turn. An hour later a woman comes out and calls me back to her office. I express my concerns about Sam's drinking and marijuana use. I tell her, "I am concerned about his drinking and marijuana use, and at times it leads to anger and property damage. I wish he would attend AA meetings."

The woman interviewing me says that Sam does not deny and admits to excessive use of alcohol. She explains, "He told me he stopped drinking and using marijuana completely at the beginning of September, after the inappropriate phone call that resulted in the Order of Protection."

The woman then changed the subject and went on to say, "Sam expressed his concerns about your mental stability. He says you live in a dream world. That you are obsessed with your dreams and you have a spiritual blog. He thinks the term *schizophrenia* describes your behaviors. He said you told him that you have a relationship with his best friend in another dimension. He said you hear the voice of God."

Of course, I had to respond to his accusations. I explained, "I have been practicing yoga and meditation for twenty years and have dedicated my life to a spiritual path. I articulate my dreams into creative writing. I obtain inspiration from my imagination and the dream world. I often dream about this man, and he has become my Muse in my writing."

O, Invisible Lover, how you trouble me so and cause me so much grief! But also, how

130

you inspire me to write and bring forth the best version of myself.

Detour

I've asked myself, *Did I make a wrong turn somewhere in life.* My life is a mess. Even my house is a mess. Is this what God intended for me? I wish I had a crystal ball, so I could look into my future and get a glimpse of where this new road I'm on is taking me.

Maybe there are no wrong turns in life- just detours. I'm learning to trust myself and to keep focused on the present. The past I cannot change, and the present is unfolding. In every new moment, a new version of me is being born. All I have to do is surrender to the process and trust God.

Who knows, maybe this moment in my life is the best detour ever. I just don't know it yet.

The Controller

I needed to text Sam about a life insurance policy I wanted to purchase on him. We own a home together, and he will be paying child support. My attorney thought this was a good idea in the very beginning. I hesitate to discuss the matter because I already know that Namah will be the one responding to my text. I suspect that Namah can't help herself and feels the need to control Sam's phone. Here's how I imagine the conversation going:

Me: I am getting a ten-year term life insurance policy at $150,000 on you since we have the house and kids. The agency needs to get your authorization. It will cost me $25 a month. If you're not willing to, I will get a court order. I hope you will cooperate. There is no medical exam.

Sam: What part of we are getting a divorce that you don't understand? It's called detachment. I want nothing to do with you unless it concerns the children — the audacity of even asking. My suggestion to you is to find another individual to ask. Please don't text me again unless it is regarding the children. Remember you have an OOP out on me. Don't be texting stuff non-kid related. You need psychological help. Plus, I have Namah take one out on me. Go to match.com and find a new meal ticket. I'm not your retirement plan.

Jaws

Everyone had a piece of advice for me
during my divorce. All I could think was,
*Really you know what it's like to be floating
in the ocean with sharks circling you;
wondering if you were going to be eaten
alive or if you do survive, pieces of you
missing.*

A life jacket will do you no good; it will
only keep your head bobbing above water.

Israel's Judgment

But let justice roll down like waters, and righteousness like an everflowing stream.
Amos 5:24

A year has passed since Sam left. I counted the times I was in and out of a courtroom last year, eight. I knew I had a restitution hearing coming up for the missing diamond earring. My attendance was not required, and so I opted not to miss another day of work.

When my attorney called, Carol, I was taken by surprise. I forgot about the hearing and the fate awaiting me, holding me financially responsible for the illusive earring. When I answered the phone, Carol exclaimed, "I won it!"

I couldn't comprehend at first what she was talking about. It took me all of three seconds to remember the hearing was today. I replied hesitantly, "So now what?"

Carol explained, "I am going to motion to have your case dismissed today. Lay low until it is. Stay away from Namah until this is over. She might try to trap you still. On the stand, I tore her apart. Namah had claimed that her earring was worth $5300 and that she had no receipt for it because it was a gift from a friend in Israel. She only produced two estimates from jewelers. I asked her if she had a photo of the earring, and of course, she did not."

I suddenly remembered the attempt Sam had made the night before to get me on the phone. I told Carol about how he called my son's cell phone and asked to speak to me. I had a feeling that told me not to. The Order of Protection only allows texting or emailing as a form of communication. Her response was, "Good thing you didn't talk to him. It could have been a trap."

I thanked her for all her help and told her she was an angel.

Many Uncertainties

Today has been like every other day for the past year. I wake up panic-stricken wondering what emergency I am going to face today. Is my minivan going to break down again? Am I going to get more court papers in the mail? Will there be more threatening, belittling text messages? Am I going to feel alienated by another friend or family member? Will I feel like crawling in a deep, dark hole? Or will I have enough strength in me to pull myself up, face my day and all the what-ifs that are now my norm?

And without a second thought, I get up because my kids need me. And I will be damn if a jezebel* raises my kids!

*Jezebel is a figure in the Hebrew Bible. She was the wife of Ahab. She became associated with false prophets and pressed the cult of Baal on the Israelite kingdom. She finally met her demise when eaten alive by dogs.

The Flying Monkeys

It's bad enough being constantly bombarded by ongoing text messages from Namah; now she has recruited her entourage as well, and converted them to her religion. They now troll me on the internet. I find their lovely comments that are meant to cause me confusion, anger, and grief, and instead of reacting, I delete and block them. I'm sure this pisses them off.

The flying monkeys want to drive you crazy. It's like they get off on it. Meredith Miller with Inner Integration gives this advice for dealing with flying monkeys, she says, "Stay in integrity. Opt out and go no contact. Block them on social media. And don't try to convince them of the truth. It never works."

Lions, and tigers, and bears. Oh my! Lions, and tigers, and bears, and flying monkeys?! WTF?!

A Month Ago

A month ago, marked a year since Sam left. I bought a bottle of Sangria on my way home from work. The last time I drank any drop of alcohol was on my birthday last year. That was also the day I filed my Response to his petition for divorce. It didn't feel real then, and it doesn't feel real now.

A month ago, my minivan broke down again. This is the third time in less than a year. It broke down in the same spot as last time, a block from the kid's school. It is the ECU my mechanic tells me. I replaced this part last summer. I saved money by purchasing the part from a company in Florida instead of going through the dealership. This would turn out to be a big mistake. At least I bought a lifetime warranty on the part, but a month has gone by, and still, my minivan is sitting at my mechanic's, waiting on the replacement part. In the meantime, I am borrowing my mom Sue's car. Thank God for my folks!

A month ago, is when the pain started. On the morning of the Super Blood Blue Moon, I swooped up my daughter out of her bed and carried her outside to see the rare event. Big mistake! The pain is unbearable. It burns like the pain from a cesarean (which I had with both of my kids). My leg and arm muscles have cramped up. I have tingling in my hands and feet. I know something is seriously wrong.

My Letter to God

O Lord, no wonder you have so few friends when you treat them so hard. St. Theresa

Dear God,

I am mad at you! Just when I thought I survived the worst parts of my divorce, now my body is failing me! I do not accept this! What good am I to my children if I am not able to care and provide for them?

For your name's sake, have mercy on me, Lord! I've dedicated my life to you. I have remained steadfast in my devotion to you. But you already know my heart and know that I am willing to risk losing everything for you. Is that why now my health has been compromised?

All I can focus on is my pain. It consumes my thoughts during my waking hours. I cannot live like this! Please, God, I need answers. I need to know my body will heal and I can be fixed. I am scared to think I have to endure this much longer.

If this is the devil's doing, tell him he's wasting his time. I have always needed you and need you now and forever. My faith is stronger than it's ever been.

But God, if this is a test from you, please know Father, that when I regain my health, I will continue to do my best to honor you. But God, if you want the world to know my story, then I ask you to restore my body.

I don't know if it's the closeness I feel to death right now or the pain that makes me brave, but today Lord I shared with a dying woman that I met you. She was gracious and deeply moved by my words. I reassured her that there is nothing to fear in death. The fear in her eyes diminished and swelling up in me was a lightness that I can only describe as a sign of your presence. I felt you in me and all around me.

I have survived a year of pure hell! My work isn't finished. I'm only getting started. Thank you for all your blessings during this time in my life. Right now, I need another miracle!

All my Love,

Me

Assholes

Someone should put a sensor on my mouth!

When I was on the phone with the city reporting illegal dumping in front of my house, the woman remarked, "I don't know why people do that?"

I responded by saying, "Because they are assholes." She laughed.

I like the word asshole. It describes most of the people I have to deal with in sucky situations. I use it a lot when I'm driving, and some asshole isn't paying attention to the light that just turned green. He/she is on their damn phone texting or talking. And I shout, "Go asshole!"

Or when I'm dealing with Sam, and it takes him six months to give me the title to my minivan that was court ordered to me. He knows damn well I want to sell it and get something more reliable for the kids and me. I think, *God what an asshole!*

And then I get the title, and Namah's name is a lien holder on the title. I think, *Damn she's an asshole!*

If I didn't pray and meditate every day, I would be a giant asshole.

Black Beauty

"Look for the helpers. You will always find people who are helping." – Fred Rogers

I was referred to Scott by Harry. Scott reached out to me in an email and introduced himself. "Hello M, Harry's request is very important to me, so I would like to help you any way I can. Is it ok if I call you tomorrow to discuss?"

In my email, to Scott, I tell him, "I am looking for a 2006-10 SUV or pick up 2WD. I like Chevy and Ford. Will consider a Toyota. **DO NOT** want a Dodge. I need space for me, my two kids, and two dogs. Also, don't care for fancy gadgets- like simple. I look forward to your phone call."

Two weeks later Scott called me and said, "M a client of ours just brought in their 2007 Tahoe. There are only 111,100 miles on it. It's been well maintained, and I think you will like it."

Without even seeing it I anxiously told Scott I wanted it. My son's birthday was approaching. I teased him saying, "For your birthday you're getting a Tahoe!"

My excitement quickly dwindled when I realized my minivan wasn't running. When I got it back from my mechanic, I refused to drive it. So, for three weeks it just sat in my driveway. I was regularly starting the engine and letting it run, but one morning the engine didn't turn over. I thought, Oh Crap!

I cleaned everything out of the minivan. I tried to start it- hoping for a miracle, but no such luck. I popped the hood and looked at the battery terminals and noticed there was some corrosion. I poured some white vinegar into a plastic container and, with a toothbrush, I scrubbed off the corrosion from the battery. I borrowed my dad's battery charger and charged it for a couple of hours. To my astonishment, the minivan started right up! I shouted, "Thank you, Jesus!"

Lo and behold on my son's birthday Scott delivered the Tahoe to my doorstep! Scott's partner drove away my minivan. I was so elated to see it go; I wanted to cry. Scott was a blessing and, he went beyond any expectations I had. He kept his word. My trade in value was more than what I expected, my payments were within my monthly budget, and my needs were met in a timely fashion.

Give Me the Headline

Man On the Run! A white male, age 40-50 was arrested on Passover. A domestic dispute broke out at his girlfriend's residence at 66 South Baal Street. The girlfriend, Namah called the cops during a heated argument and a night of drinking and reported to the police property damage. When the cops arrived, the suspect was reported to be on foot avoiding arrest. The suspect was found and placed under arrest. The man spent the night in jail. The judge ordered him to attend Anger Management and AA meetings.

Not an Easter Picnic

For the first time in years, I plan an Easter feast. On the menu: Bacon Egg Casserole, Tatortot Casserole, Slow cooked pulled pork on Hawaiian buns, and for desert Pineapple Coconut Cake.

I wanted the day to be perfect. After the traumatic experience, my kids had to go through on Passover, witnessing their father being arrested, I was determined that this Easter would be the start of a new family tradition.

When my folks arrived with my kids, I was eager just to hug them and smell their little heads. I do this often. My dad and Mom Sue were hungry, so I made their plates right away. The kids had a late breakfast. I told them they could eat later. They binged on Easter candy as I ate the wonderful meal I spent hours preparing.

After my folks were finished and praised my cooking, they dropped a bomb on me. My dad went first. "Do you know how I went to the heart Doctor a month ago? It turns out I have to have open heart surgery. I'm going to schedule it in July or August. And your mom has some news."

I asked, "Is it worse than the news you gave me?"

My mom Sue dishearteningly replied, "I'm afraid so. I have aggressive bladder cancer. The doctor told me I have two choices: they can cut out the cancer and do chemo treatments or remove the bladder all together and I will still have to have the chemo. With the first option, there's a 50-60% chance of the cancer returning."

I was dumbfounded. I said, "So this past week you both found out that you need surgery? And to top it off you had to deal with my news about Sam getting arrested."

All they could say was, "Yep."

My dad finished by saying, "We decided to take care of mom's surgery first so that I can take care of her, and when she's better, I will have my surgery."

I was shocked by the news. It wasn't until the next day when I was waiting for my kids at their school to pick them up, that it hit me. I was talking to my friend Anna on the phone. She's been my go-to person from the

150

very beginning. She lives out of state, so I can tell her all the details of my divorce, and I don't worry about it coming back around to me through the beehive.

I told her the events that had transpired on Easter and the news my folks broke to me. And that's when it hit me. I knew my dad would be fine, but my mom Sue may not. I told Anna tearfully," I went from adoring this woman when I was a kid. I'd go to her house, and she'd put on puppet shows in her window. All the kids in the neighborhood loved her. Then as a teenager, when she became my stepmom, I hated her. Now I've come full circle and I love her. I can't imagine my life without her."

Tears were flowing from my eyes, and my thoughts went to my dad. "How can my dad live without her?" I expressed to Anna.

All Anna could say was, "I'm sorry M. I will add them to my prayer list."

No Coffee!

It is week two with no coffee. My physical therapist, Tara, has me only drinking water to reset my bladder.

When I first met her, I was skeptical that she could help me. On the day she examined me, I told her I pulled a muscle carrying my sixty-pound daughter outside to see the Super Moon. She read over the report from the pelvic pain doctor in front of her. Tara then examined me on her table. This required me to undress from the waist down. As she did her examination, I closed my eyes. Tara said, "Take a deep breath in through your nose and out through your mouth."

With my eyes closed and my hands on my abdomen, I did as she instructed. It was all of a sudden that I saw an image of her in my mind's eye. In the image, she was wearing a white veil and dressed like a novice nun. The image only lasted a few seconds.

After she did her internal examination, she then placed her hands on my abdomen. Her touch was light, and I could feel the heat from her hands.

When she finished, I asked her, "Have you heard of Reiki?"

Tara replied, "Yes, what I'm doing is kind of the same."

She then had me get dressed and when she returned she said, "I think I can help you. During my exam, I felt your pelvic muscles spasm on the left side where you said you're experiencing a lot of pain. You have no pelvic floor support. I want you just to drink water and urinate every two hours. Also, only gentle yoga."

"For how long?" I inquired, wondering how much longer I had to survive my mornings without coffee and now no juice or almond milk.

"As long as it takes. Also, no sex." Tara added.

With a laugh, I said, "Well that won't be a problem."

I was confident Tara could help me because of the vision I had of her. I felt comfortable with her, and I was willing to sacrifice my coffee to get 100% better. Whatever it takes!

Oh Soul, My Soul

The following took place in the early hours on May 13, 2018 (Mother's Day) during the half- asleep and half-awake state:

This morning I listened to my soul as she cried out in pain. She tells me, "This is not what I wanted. Why did he have to leave like that? I miss him. I wish things were different."

She sobs and sobs and sobs. And moans and moans and moans. When I fully awake and become aware of her grief, her turmoil, I cry with her, for her. There is no one here to comfort her but me.

500 Days

If you want to turn your life around, try thankfulness. It will change your life mightily. -Gerald Good

It's been 500 days since that cold night in January. I was a damn mess and still am! The days continue to pass in slow motion, and they feel like an eternity. I have restless nights haunted by nightmares, anxiety attacks throughout my days, and constant fatigue from the lack of sleep and the stress I am under.

But every day I manage to pray, meditate, and do yoga. I listen to my favorite minister, Joyce Meyer, on YouTube and recently got hooked on the inspirational words of Abraham Hicks. Her messages are about aligning your thoughts with Source Energy. For example, in her book, *Co-creating at Its Best*, she says, "When you feel the way Source feels about someone, you're in sync with Source. You may call it forgiveness; we call it alignment. And you get hooked on that feeling because it sure feels better to love them than to hate them." This I have to remind myself of often.

It wasn't until May, four months after Sam left that I was able to remove Sam's wedding band from my finger. I remember I took it off right before I left to visit family in Illinois. I had this stupid thought in my head. What if I meet a cute guy while I'm there? Once there, I was just so glad to be around my two favorite cousins and family that the thought of hooking up with someone never entered my mind again.

In September, I packed up the remainder of Sam's clothes, pictures, and miscellaneous belongings and put them in the garage. Sam spent a lot of time out there working on cars. His hot rod still sits there, waiting for him to come to get it, along with all his tools. I avoid going in there unless I need something. It is the one place I can still feel his presence.

And then before the holidays, I threw away all his love letters and cards he gave me over the years. On New Year's Eve, I invited all the kids over from the street for a marshmallow roast. I burned all our old files and outdated documents and put Sam's files that looked important in the garage for safe keeping.

Now I just sit here and wait. The judge is going to make his final decision on the child support and the house, whether or not the kids and I can continue to live here. I am scared, this I can admit. But there's only one direction to move in life, and that is forward. So, forward it is with an attitude of gratitude and a spirit of hope that one day my dreams will come true and I will feel whole again.

June 19

Pray without ceasing. -1 Thessalonians 5:17

I am at work when I get the call from my attorney. I answer her call with hesitation. On the other end Faith says, "Hi M, the judge has ruled on your case."

I humbly ask, "So is it good or bad news?"

She replies, "Well both. Child support was awarded to you monthly and retroactive support for last year. Also, he will have to pay your attorney fees."

I interrupted her and asked, "But what about the house?"

She responded disheartened, "Well the judge ordered for you to refinance the house in 120 days or sell it."

My eyes teared up, and I quickly remarked, "I didn't care about the other stuff. I only cared about the house. Can I appeal the judge's decision?"

She answered, "Yes you can, but I don't do appeals."

I choked back the tears when I hung up the phone. I wanted to cry, but I was taking care of a client. I would have to wait until I was in my Tahoe, alone, with my sunglasses on.

I ended up stopping at the grocery store on my way home. I called my dear friend Anna to vent. I was enraged! She answered her phone, and I yell, "I fucking hate him! I've never hated someone so much as I hate him!"

I explained the judge's decision to her. Anna calmly said, "M you have every right to feel rage towards him. But remember God is on your side and I really feel everything is going to be alright. Everything will work out in your best interest because He knows what's best for you and you don't."

I agreed with her. God's been with me since the beginning of this storm. Why would He abandon me now? I recognize that I lack faith when I need to trust Him and now I've allowed fear to enter my mind. This I need to pray about.

July 3

My client Harry referred me to an appeals attorney. I arrange to see her before I go out of town for the Fourth of July. Her name is Helaina, and she is a fire burning hell. She is all business. I am a bit intimidated by her demeanor. When she enters the conference room, I shake her hand, and her handshake is firm. She explains, "I've read over the Rule 69 Agreement and the judge's ruling on your divorce that Harry sent to me. It is not the decree like you thought." She then asks, "What is your main concern and how can I help you?"

I tell her about the house and how the judge ordered me to refinance in 120 days or sell it. I ask her, "Can I appeal the judge's decision on the house?"

Her reply infuriated me. She said, "Unfortunately you will have no luck with the house. It looks like you and your husband agreed to be Tenants in Common, but there were no terms set." She then rolled her eyes and said, "The judge is an idiot. He threw out your agreement that you and your husband made."

I then told her about the child support payments not being fair because Sam did not produce current financial records or a Schedule K on his partnership. Helaina requested any documentation that I had on the partnership. I had the ACC records with me and handed them to her. She quickly glanced at them and remarked, "He formed this partnership in 2016 when you were still together and married. This is an undivided asset that you're entitled to half of. How did your lawyer miss this?"

Again, I am enraged but remain calm. I relied on my lawyer for all her expertise. How did she not catch this? Helaina says firmly, "Well this is the leverage you can use to negotiate your house." I thank her for her time and charge the $450 for the hour I was there to my credit card. I leave feeling more hopeful than before.

I call my lawyer right away and tell her what the appeals attorney told me. Faith responded eagerly to proceed with negotiating an agreement with Sam and his attorney. What Faith presented was an agreement that gave me 75% equity in the home and four more years to stay and raise our children. In exchange, I would relinquish any interest in his partnership. Sam did not take the deal. Faith then made a plea with

161

the court for a hearing regarding the undivided asset. I felt if the judge granted me a hearing, that would be enough to change Sam's mind and he would reconsider my offer. My gut told me Sam does not want to go back to court.

Judge Deadhead's Decision

It is the end of October, and I've not heard anything regarding the plea. I call Faith and ask her if she can find out what's taking so long. She calls me back, two days later, and tells me, "The judge confused the plea with the decree, and not as two separate issues."

I think, Oh brother! There is no light on in this judge's intellect. He's what I refer to as *Sleepers or Zombies.* These are people who go through life unconscious. They are not fully present (meaning living in the now) and therefore lack empathy, compassion, and the ability to use the power of their awareness to make right choices or they miss opportunities because they are not paying attention. They do the minimum required of them because their minds are often somewhere else; either making future plans, trying to escape the present, or reliving the past.

One week goes by, and I get the news. Judge Deadhead denies a hearing and does not enter into court records Sam's partnership as an *undivided asset*. I'm screwed! Now I can wear a label that reads: **Displaced Homemaker**. A list of qualifications: at least 30 years old, has not worked as an employee for a substantial number of years but has worked in his or her home providing unpaid services for family members, has been dependent on the income of another family member but is no longer being supported by that income, has been receiving public welfare assistance for having dependent children, and is underemployed and finding it difficult to upgrade employment.

My Silent Prayer

In the darkened silence I heard my wordless prayer. *God, I would ask that you strike down my ex-husband! Shoot, that's no good, the children still need a father. Lord, I then request that he suffers greatly with a disease or cancer! No, that won't do. I'm afraid I'd be the one to take care of him for the sake of the children. Father-God, I simply ask then that he goes bald, becomes toothless, and a can't have an erection! Amen.*

See Through the Illusion

I have come to the painful conclusion that no one is to blame but me for the harsh reality I endured these past two years. I thought by staying in an unhappy, unhealthy marriage was what God expected of me. That the sacrifice I had to make as a mother and woman of God made me more righteous. I now understand that it wasn't love that kept me in my marriage, but fear. And, God desires me to be happy, whole, and in a loving relationship. The following excerpt is from *gnosticteachings.org, Evolution of Sex: Where We Are Now*. I hope, as women, we begin to make better choices in the men we commit our lives to, use and trust our intuition, and lean on God when we need Him.

We all have an idea of what a person is like and who they are, and perhaps through experience, some years, our concept of that person may be based on certain experiences that we have had with them, but it is not based upon all our experiences with them (since we select only certain experiences to use in that concept), and it certainly is not based on all of their experiences since we have only seen a fraction of their experiences, and only been told a select few of their experiences. So, our concept of each person is based only on a few select impressions, and from that, we build an idea of that person. Eventually, a day comes when they do something that does not fit our idea of that person, and we are shocked, overwhelmed, surprised. Perhaps we fight with them or end the relationship. Yet whose fault is it? It is ours, because we built an illusion in our mind of that person, someone we thought we knew. But really, we only saw the lie we were telling ourselves about that person, we never saw the reality of that person, the truth. If we are capable of that amount of self-deception with some tangible, perceptible phenomena in our immediate environment, how could we possibly have any idea about God... whom few if any of us have actually experienced? Yet everyone has the conviction of belief, the concept, the idea that we have some notion of what God is, and we hold to that, thinking it is true. Meanwhile, the reality is that we do not see reality.

Surviving Divorce with Mindfulness

Mindfulness is a door that lets you out of the stuffy room of rumination, worry, anger, and anxiety, and into the fresh air of the here and now, into a more compassionate and healthy life. -Sameet M. Kumar Ph.D

Being mindful throughout your day helps you develop healthy habits, practice patience with tolerance, and connect with Spirit. The past two years have taught me how important it is to yield to my emotional, mental, and physical needs in order to move forward with grace and brave the unknown. The habits I have developed over the past two decades has improved my quality and experience of daily life. I would like to share with you, my reader, the things that have worked for me.

I keep a planner for my daily appointments and things I need to do. Simply reminding myself what time to pick up the kids from school, helps me stay on track throughout my day. This was a tremendous help during my divorce because I was emotionally overwhelmed and would forget the simplest things, like trash day and bills that are due, but having it written down minimized the stress.

I also begin each day with yoga. This would set the tone for my day. It strengthens the mind, body, and soul. Often I play music in the background. Some of my favorites to listen to are: Casting Crowns, Lifehouse, Rob Thomas, Dido, Mufford & Sons, and Christine Perri. It's like putting on armor before you face the day with all of its challenges.

Throughout my day I am faced with challenges regarding anxiety and anger. What's helped me, if I'm driving, is to take deep breaths; counting to four, holding for four, and releasing for four. If I am able to go for a walk, I apply the same technique. Often your anger and anxiety are trying to tell you something. Ask yourself, *What needs to change? What am I frustrated about?* You can also redirect your thoughts and focus on a happy memory to calm yourself. Take the time to breathe, pause, and observe these feelings to bring yourself back into realignment with Source Energy (God, the Divine).

Maintaining a healthy diet is so important. During my divorce, I didn't even have an appetite, but I always eat eggs, or I have a bowl of granola with a banana. I take vitamins before I leave the house in the morning. I also always take water and a snack (sun chips, cereal bar, or trail mix) with me. I mainly drink water throughout my day, and this helps my mind and body function better. For lunch, I will eat a sandwich with deli meat and cheese on whole grain with a cup of yogurt and fresh fruit. In the evening I normally eat salad with my main meal. I do not snack after 6 pm and stop drinking water 2 hours before bedtime.

Praying is something I do throughout my day. I pray in the shower, before a meal, in the car, whenever the need arises. I pray for my loved ones, my children, my enemies, and humanity as a whole. I remind myself that there is always someone suffering more than me in the world. We all have our cross to bear, but with God, our burdens are lighter.

Journaling is also a tool I use to connect with my intuition. Every day I find time to write down my thoughts or my dreams from the previous night. Later, I can read it, and discover what areas I need to work on or see the progress I have made. I don't judge my feelings or my thoughts; I am simply a witness to my unfolding and becoming.

Staying connected to family and friends that love you is so important. My Sunday ritual is now spending time with my dad and my mom Sue. I give them an update on my week over a meal that my dad has prepared. We have grown closer, and I look forward to our time together.

Having a good attitude about yourself does affect your mood and how others perceive and react to you. Repeating affirmations in the mirror is very helpful. Two of my favorites are, *I love to be loved, and I accept myself as I am.* They are written in my daughter's handwriting and taped to my mirror.

I spend my free time with my kids, reading a good book, listening to educational and inspirational YouTube videos, or writing in my journal. Recently I enrolled in a Tai Chi class. I am always exploring new things that aid in my wellbeing. The books I read are from the library. The class is through the Parks and Recreations. Reading is free and my class for six weeks is just $20!

Striving to be the best version of yourself during the storms in your life takes grace. God's grace is abundant, and with discipline and dedication to mindfulness, you will begin to transform on the inside, and your outer life will align with your inner. You can expect many upsets and disharmony when you're living a spiritual life centered on God; this is because He is making way for you to receive His blessings. The old must be discarded for it no longer serves you. *Ephesians 4:22 Continue to remain in faith through the darkness and keep your thoughts on your Heavenly Father, and I can promise you all will be well.*

The Mantra of Believing and Receiving

I believe. I receive. I believe. I receive.
I believe. I receive. I believe. I receive.
I believe. I receive. I believe. I receive.
I believe. I receive. I believe. I receive.
I believe. I receive. I believe. I receive.
I believe. I receive. I believe. I receive.
I believe. I receive. I believe. I receive.
I believe. I receive. I believe. I receive.
I believe. I receive. I believe. I receive.
I believe. I receive. I believe. I receive.
I believe. I receive. I believe. I receive.
I believe. I receive. I believe. I receive.
I believe. I receive. I believe. I receive.
I believe. I receive. I believe. I receive.
I believe. I receive. I believe. I receive.

Final Thoughts

Weeping may endure for a night, but joy comes in the morning. -Psalm 30:5b

I could've glossed over my divorce with manicures, wine, and dating sites. I could've jumped into another relationship right away as a means of a temporary escape. I could've also completely lost control of myself and given up on life. Or I could write a book about it, do the deep inner work to heal my wounds, and shed the wife. It was the scariest journey I have ever been on. The discoveries I made about myself are both painful and awe-inspiring.

If someone snapped a picture of me to memorialize my divorce, it would be of me on my prayer mat, humbly on my knees, with tears streaming down my face. You'd hear the desperate pleas of a broken woman begging God to get her through just one more day. And He did! Every single day He did. He answered every single prayer.

I know I am in God's favor. I know God has a purpose for my life and He desperately wants me to share my story with the world. There will be many women who will be able to relate to my story. And this deeply saddens me. But I hope my story gives you strength. God is faithful and always listening to your prayers. He is guiding you, if you let Him, to your destination.

I cannot stress enough how important dream work is and how important it is to let your life unfold according to God's timing. Everything you are going through has a purpose.

Change is slow, but you can do all things through the *Spirit* because He is your strength, abundance is His favor, and mercy is His gift. His love is everlasting. Seek Him with all your mind, body, and soul, and your life will be blessed!

The Dreams

Go not abroad; retire into thyself, for truth dwells in the inner man. –St. Augustine

Journaling Your Dreams

For over twenty years I have been doing dream work. It is now a passion of mine. Every morning, and frequently in the middle of the night, I write down my dream- the setting, the colors, the feeling, the people involved, the dialogue, as much detail as possible. I then have a dream book, *The Mystical Magical Marvelous World of Dreams*, that I use to interpret each symbol.

Over the years, as I've worked with my dreams, I've learned which dreams are literal or symbolic, and which are from my Higher Self (light, love) or the ego (fear based). When I dissect a dream, it gives me insight into myself (my thoughts, emotions, fears, and desires). I then can make a wise decision based on the interpretation of the dream and what is the best course of action to take in my life. They can be small decisions to life-altering decisions. But I always choose what's best that serves my Higher Self.

Dreams are one of the ways *Spirit* communicates with you. Dreams are valuable, and they offer insight into your emotional and mental state. They can be a

179

tool to guide you through the storms of your life. They can provide insights into relationships, career paths, and point out your ego flaws. Working with your dreams gives you an edge. They can prepare you for a disaster or warn you of illness. The ultimate goal of dream work is tuning into the spiritual world for guidance with the long-term goal of preparing for one's death and the next life that awaits you. If you can master the dream world, you will master this reality.

* The interpretation of dream symbols can also be found at www.dreamoods.com or www.dreambible.com

Warning of Prophetic Storm

8/13/14

I am a little girl with my dad and brother. Our house is on a mountain. My dad is working outside by his garage with his table saw. I see the clouds in the sky moving fast and dancing in a way that I've never seen before. I yell for my dad. He looks up. I then see rain down in the valley below. I tell my dad to come inside. There's no time to put his things away.

Suddenly, I see a great flood in the valley. It is washing everything away in its path. It is coming towards us, up the mountain. I tell my dad to come inside again. I am shocked by the storm-lightning flashes.

The home represents my home as a child, and the situation I find myself in now is the same I experienced then. Standing on top of the mountain represents a spiritual dream with many obstacles to overcome. The clouds are my thoughts and prayers that are taking shape. The storm coming towards me is a forewarning of emotional turmoil and needed cleansing coming my way. A storm of tears is about to break loose with rapid changes ahead. The flood will wipe everything clean, and I will be able to make a fresh start. Lightning represents a shocking turn of events. Many forces are governing my life that is beyond my control.

At the age of 9, my father and mother divorced. I took the dream as a warning of a similar major event in my own life that will happen. I believe that my faith is the mountain and I would need to be centered in God to survive the oncoming storm. It would come swiftly and destroy everything in its path. But it would be a period of cleansing and healing. My thoughts, represented by the clouds, were now manifesting and creating my reality. My inner world is longing to emerge and is joining with the outer.
#The Split

A Nun

1/3/17

I'm in a third world country disguised as a nun. There are nuns all around me. One woman has long dreads. We are in a convent hiding. We are trying to escape the country.

The nun represents my unhappiness in my life. I am looking for an escape. The convent is my need for spiritual support. The woman with dreadlocks represents how I go against the norm in society.

In my present life, I am not happy. My husband, my friends, and those around me do not offer me the spiritual support I need. I want to escape, but I am afraid.

Note to Reader: Husband left 1/15/17

House Flood

3/21/17

My dad, my brother, and I are at our old house on Orange Drive that I lived in as a teenager. The house has been torn down, but the foundation remains. I walk through the house. There is a picture window. When I look through it, I see the most beautiful view of vines, trees, and greenery. My brother is acting like he has a grudge. Dad says he'll buy it and fix it up for him. My brother says firmly, "No."

I think I would love it. All of a sudden flood waters come rushing in. We run for it. We climb stairs and move through more abandoned buildings. We are trapped! We make it somewhere that we can jump down and get away.

The house represents a state of consciousness that I am moving away from. It being abandoned represents leaving the past behind me. The window and my view of the world represent my outlook on my life. It being a large window represents my openness to new experiences. The foundation represents my belief system that is still intact. The greenery and vegetation are my new start in life and the healing forces involved with my situation. The flood waters rising are the overwhelmed emotions I am feeling right now. My brother, being negative, also represents the part of me that is also negative.

I am leaving one world behind and moving forward in life. My dad is there to support me. When I was a teenager and moved out of my dad's home, I very much looked forward to a new life.

Yoga and Shiny Things

4/4/17

I am in a car trying to reach a yoga studio. I reach it, and there is a lot of sand. It is in a secluded beach area. There is a woman there. She is the instructor.

My best friend and I join in for yoga. We are told to hold hands. We begin with arm warm-ups. My friend is told by a woman that she is beautiful but needs to go to the doctor.

My friend tells me, "Men are seduced by nice things. When they surround themselves with friends who have lust in their hearts for power, wealth, and women; it will lead them astray."

The beach is symbolic of the meeting between two states of mind. The sand represents my shift in perspective about my marriage and the mental processes involved. The water symbolizes the emotional processes involved. With yoga as my spiritual practice, I will able to balance my mind, heart, and body to adapt to the coming changes in my life. My friend's message sheds light on human nature in general and how easily men or women can be led away from God.

I do end up going to a doctor for female problems. I am told I need a hysterectomy. I decide to change my diet and work on healing my body instead.

*excerpt from madisonmeadows.blogspot

Fire, Call 999!

5/2/17

There is a fire in the fire department. I dialed 999 for help. I am one of the firefighters putting out the fire. I am soaking wet, but we manage to put out the fire.

I am experiencing a period of cleansing. Fire is symbolic of my inner transformation. Something old is passing away, and something new is entering my life. My thoughts and views will change. Firefighters are a symbol of hope. By putting out the fire, I will overcome my obstacles with much effort.

The number 999 means certain aspects of my life are ending. An important phase is coming to an end. What is happening is for karmic reasons, which will become known in the near future. It is clearing the way for me to pursue my life's purpose and soul mission. I will be guided by the angels. I must devote myself to my life's mission. Expect many closures in my life- family, friends, work, and home life; for this is preparing me to begin a wonderful new life and lifestyle.

Jesus, My Helper

6/14/17

I am running up a flight of stairs from a demon. At the top of the staircase is Jesus. He extends his arm as to say, *"Take courage and stand with Me."* He took a stance of power and directed me to stand next to Him. He spoke no words, but he conveyed to me, *"I got this. Trust and believe in Me."* I stood with Him no longer afraid.

As my court date approaches for my divorce, I have been depressed, worried, and afraid. I worry about whether or not I will be able to stay in my home, my new financial responsibilities, and my children's wellbeing. I have been praying for help, guidance, and strength. Up until I had this dream I felt completely abandoned by God. **And I will pray the Father, and He will give you another Helper, that He may abide with you forever. John 14:16**

Before I fell asleep, I did a meditation. It is part of my nightly routine to quiet my mind as I am lying in bed. I close my eyes and review my day. Generally, I drift off to sleep during this process. Suddenly I heard a loud knock from inside my head. It was a *knock, knock, knock*. My instant thought was what is my subconscious trying to tell me?

Behold, I stand at the door and knock, if anyone hears My voice and opens the door, I will come into him and will dine with him, and he with me. Revelation 3:20

The dream reminded me that I am not alone. Jesus is with me. He is my Helper. All I need to do is completely trust Him. **Be strong and courageous. Do not be afraid or terrified because of them, for the Lord Your God goes with you; he will never leave you or forsake you. Deuteronomy 31:6**

*excerpt from madisonmeadows.blogspot

Angel

7/5/17

My friend, Angel, had cut her hair like mine. I commented and asked her if she missed her long hair. She said she finally got used to her short hair and liked it. She flirted with a guy. I watched her flirt and thought she was good at it.

What I remember about my friend Angel, she was single and dating. I always thought she had a lot of game when it came to flirting. She had long hair when I knew her. Her cutting her hair represents drastic changes to my approach in life regarding dating since hair has to do with sexual virility and sensuality.

Recently I joined a dating website. I feel that my friend represents the qualities I liked in her when it comes to her flirtatious nature. After 19 years of being with one man, I am a bit nervous about putting myself out there. I feel the need to create new energy in my life. I don't want to be angry anymore.

Note to Reader: My friend Angel passed away from ALS and often comes to me in my dreams.

The Devil

7/8/17

I zoomed upwards into the sky. I hear the devil. He is laughing and speaks to me. I tell him I am in love and that's never going to change. He laughs again and says, "Pick a number then divide it by two." I pick four. He says, "It's five," and laughs some more. I wasn't scared.

The devil represents the temptations that I will encounter. The evil laugh is the feelings I feel of hopelessness and that the enemy is working against me. Four represents how I get things done and materialistic matters. Five represents action and the five senses.

The devil will use trickery and many devices to trap you. I rely on my sixth sense for guidance and to navigate the many landmines that the enemy has laid. I remind myself that soon this will be over and my life will be better. Until then I pray a lot. I will never denounce God. And I will profess my love for Him in all my trials and tribulations.

An Earthquake

9/13/17

I am standing outside of my childhood home. The earth is quaking. Trees are being uprooted. It is moving towards the house and will destroy it and everything in its path. I want to run back and get the vehicle parked in the driveway. It's too late.

My childhood home represents the situation I find myself in is the same in which I am now experiencing. The earthquake represents a major shake-up that is threatening my stability. The uprooted trees are old belief systems that no longer serve me.

I was nine years old when my parents separated and divorced. It was a tough time for me and turned my world upside down. The emotional turmoil I kept to myself, and slowly I fell into a depression that would last for years.

Fortunately, now that I am older and wiser, I understand that as devastating as my divorce is I am not resistant to the changes in my life and trust that God will get me through this and ultimately my life will be better.

A Gas Station

9/22/17

I'm in a gas station. I order a cantaloupe smoothie. I pay with my debit card and wait for the cashier to return me my card.

The gas station represents my need to reenergize myself. I am running on low energy and need to take time to refuel. The cantaloupe represents the tough image I put forth, but I am sensitive on the inside. It being a smoothie suggests I will have a smooth road ahead. **#Forty Winks**

The Gypsy Fortune Teller

10/6/17

**A woman tells me that she can see
spirits and talk to them. She speaks to a
spirit named Claudia. She delivers
several messages to me and warns me
about my health, "Slow down, and you'll
be okay. If you don't, you won't be
okay. You're materialistic. Your book is
going to do really well. I've been
following you many lifetimes. You
always write."**

At the time my health was fine. Yes, I was
stressed, fatigued, and sleeping poorly.
Three months later, however, I would find
myself struggling just to keep up with my
daily duties. When I pulled my lower
abdomen muscle, the pain was so severe,
almost crippling, I couldn't do my normal
activities and was forced to slow down.
Walking became difficult because my legs
would cramp up and I often felt lightheaded
with tingling sensations throughout my
whole body.

I was told by the pelvic pain specialist that
because I had two cesareans that the scar

tissue and nerves around the strained muscle had contributed to my problems. It would be a long road to recovery. The dream reminded me that I had to slow down if I was going to get through this. So, with physical therapy, gentle yoga, reiki, and prayer, I slowly restored my body and am still on the road to recovery. I'm learning to listen to my body more closely and tune into the physical changes that come with aging. **#A Month Ago #No Coffee!**

Gangsters

1/14/18

Gangsters killed a bunch of people. I pretend I'm dead and hide under a sheet. I am pushed down a hole and try to climb out. I'm left for dead.

Gangsters represent overwhelming circumstances in my life. I feel I am being ganged up on. The murder of others represents deep-seated anger towards others. Hiding represents that I'm looking for a sense of protection and security. A hole represents how I feel stuck. By climbing out, I am trying to overcome a great struggle.

This dream has to do with my anger. I feel stuck in this emotion. I don't want to feel this way, but I feel like I am under attack and desperately want security/protection. I recognize this overwhelming powerful emotion and am determined to overcome it.

Sam Collapsing

2/11/18

Sam collapsed on the floor in his kitchen. I went to him and yelled his name and shook him until he came to. He commented, "I see it in you too."

Soon after this dream, I would end up in the hospital. The dream forewarns of the danger to my body from my injury and also to the mental exhaustion and stress from the divorce. It is all taking a toll on both of us. (Keep reading. You will find out how this dream does foretell of Sam's breakdown.) ***#Give Me the Headline***

When I no longer knew if I could even walk and it felt like I was going to pass out, my mom Sue took me to the Emergency Room. All my blood work and the CT scan were normal. I leave discouraged and with no answers. All I can do is pray for now and ask God to get me through my days. I still have kids to drive to school and a paycheck to earn to pay the bills. This isn't easy.

The Dealership Referral

3/3/18

Harry was driving my minivan. His wife was in the front seat. I was in the back. We were in my hometown where I was born and raised. Harry took my minivan to his mechanic and got it running again.

The dream takes place in my childhood town. I take care of Harry's wife. I adore both of them very much, and they treat me like family. I feel like one of their kids and trust Harry's judgment to take my minivan to his mechanic. The dealership he refers me to is full service where they do mechanical work on vehicles and also sell a wide variety of new and used vehicles. The dream reassures me I will be treated well, and I am less worried about the process of buying a vehicle from a dealership. **#Black Beauty**

A Praying Mantis

4/19/18

There is a praying mantis. I am watching it closely.

A praying mantis brings calm and peace to your life. It reminds you to think things through before you act, listen to your intuition, and trust your instincts. Be aware of your surroundings and be in tune with your emotions. Your faith will be rewarded.

This happens to be the day of my trial. This is the final court appearance I will have to make for my divorce. Any loose ends, regarding child support payments and the house, will be determined. The dream puts my mind at ease and reminds me to remain in faith. I also will be more mindful, especially today, of my testimony I give in court.

A Princess

5/26/18

I am with a group of women learning a ritual dance. One woman says I am now a princess. We are on a dance floor learning an African style dance. I love it and am having fun with these women.

The princess represents her strength to search for meaning and ways to positively deal with difficulties and personal problems. Dancing symbolizes the dance with life. I have found unity within. I am dealing with my difficulties with a new mindset.

During the past year and a half, I continued my yoga and meditation. Two of the greatest influences on me have been Joyce Meyer and Abraham-Hicks. I religiously listened to their Youtube videos every day. They have instilled in me a new mindset that empowers me by teaching where and how to focus my thoughts, so I can create the life I desire.

The Happy Anniversary Card

6/16/18

I am reading a *Happy Anniversary* card that Namah gave to Sam. It is very long. It said, "I'm so glad I invited you to my party. If it weren't for fate stepping in, we wouldn't be together. M keeps texting about the title to her minivan. You can give it to her."

She goes on to say how she desires to be well received by his family and how she's never been happier since she met him. They were celebrating their first anniversary in October.

I was furious when I woke up from this dream. It confirmed for me that he had been cheating on me because in October he was still living at home with me. I also had a very hard time getting my title to my minivan. It took me six months! And lo and behold, who was the lien holder on my title?? Yep, Namah. **#Assholes**

A Series of Bad Dreams

After I got the news about the judge's decision regarding the house, I began having awful dreams. The house was negotiated in The Early Resolution Conference. We agreed we would be Tenants in Common and I would remain in the home and raise the kids.

After he got a lawyer, Sam quickly back peddled and demanded the house be sold or refinanced in my name (let me remind you, I never had a full-time job until Sam left and I tried, but was denied for a loan). With no terms in writing at the time we formed the agreement, the judge ruled and threw out our agreement. I felt robbed, betrayed, and scared. What would happen to my kids and me? The mortgage payment is $700 a month. I rely on my neighbors for support and help. My dad now takes care of my mom Sue due to complications with her surgery, and he has yet to have his open-heart surgery. All of this is overwhelming and doesn't seem fair. The following eight dreams reflect my insecurities, doubts, and fears about the near future. **#June 19**

A Bear

6/24/18

There are two guys in a house. A bear approaches the patio door. One of the guys opens the door to see the bear and quickly closes it. The bear comes right up to the glass and is determined to break in- the men panic. My daughter and I are outside watching this happen. We run to the car to get away.

The aggressive bear is my anger. I need to face my anger and not run from it.

A Dust Storm

6/24/18

There is a very bad dust storm I'm walking through. The air is thick with dust. I'm trying to make it to my childhood home. I can see it and want to get inside safely.

The sandstorm represents my unexpressed fears and emotions of being trapped, confined, and disoriented: an overwhelming struggle, shock, and devastation, loss, and catastrophe in my life. Time is working against me. On a positive note, the storm signifies rapid changes ahead for me.

Train Derailing

6/25/18

A train derails and nearly kills me.

My life's journey has been derailed. I am experiencing problems that require me to start over.

A Shooter

6/25/18

A shooter is outside killing people. I'm hiding in an abandoned building. My dog is outside. I watch in horror as the shooter kills my dog.

The shooter represents the feeling that there are people in my life working against me. My dog represents the loss of a good friend, which I believe to be Sam. He's killed our friendship. I have to face the emotions of this loss. I'm hiding to avoid the issues and feelings that need to be dealt with. The abandoned building represents significant changes are occurring in my life and a feeling of not being able to go back to my old ways.

Kidnapping

6/26/18

Three girls are kidnapped. One is me. We escape out a window onto a swing. We run through houses where people are, and a woman asks us what we are doing. We tell her what happened.

A kidnapper represents the feeling of being in a controlling situation. Feeling forced to do something I don't want to do. A feeling that everything is going wrong. By escaping, is my eagerness and desperation to change my situation.

I don't feel I have control over the direction of my life. Sam is in control.

Sadness and Grief

6/29/18

I'm lying in my bed asleep. I can hear the neighbor kids approaching the door to knock. I think to myself how I'm going to miss hearing those footsteps. I begin crying out to God, "My house God, I can't lose my house!"

I woke up crying. The dream felt too real. I prayed to God to save my home.

France

7/1/18

I am in France. I was excited to be there. I am a kid. I ran ahead of my family and lost them. I try to remain calm. I stand and wait in one spot for them to find me.

France represents a mindset that is immersed in a situation where the highest integrity is demanded at all times. A prolonged difficult experience for the sake of honesty that needs to brought to justice. A situation where lying is unacceptable. Being lost is my way of finding myself out of that situation.

I've had this nagging thought that something was missed in the divorce. I read through every single court document. I am blown away by all the lies alleged by my husband about me and the unwillingness to disclose his income on his business. I brought up my concern about my house to a client. He referred me to an appeal's attorney. I have a meeting with her at the end of the week. **#July 3**

Flood

7/5/18

**I am swept away by a flood but
survive.**

The flood represents the rage of my
enemies. I have enemies planning to destroy
me. By surviving the flood, I will get through
this.

*Now back to our regular scheduled
programming of not so nightmarish dreams...*

You Win!

7/23/18

Sam came to see me regarding the house and says, "You win." I was in shock but very happy. He hugged me. He was cool about it.

In this dream, Sam comes to see me about the house. Neither one of us yet know the outcome of the judge's decision, but if the judge rules in my favor, it will be the leverage I want for the house that gets Sam into negotiations with his partnership.

Often dreams show a potential outcome to a situation. This is the perfect dream to use to illustrate how a person's intentions can come through in a dream, but in reality, depending on circumstances outside of your control, don't happen. Because the judge denied my request, I never get to delight in the feeling of having won. **#Judge Deadhead's Decision**

A Walking Stick

I saw a walking stick blended into his tree. He had a cute home that was decorated.

The walking stick reminds me to be patient. By being still, the proper course of action will make itself known. I should continue what I have been doing, quietly. Don't let the wrong people know my goals; don't be too trusting or open. Results are coming, but I must allow them to come in their own time. When I do allow this, I will be in a better position to grab them and use them for my benefit. I need to stay focused on myself. Prayer and meditation will bring results and benefits.

Killer Whale

12/24/2018

I am in the front yard of my childhood home. Sam is there. Water is rushing down the hillside and with it- cars. Sam is instructing a man which car to push out into the waters and get rid of next. I am standing on the hillside in the waters holding on to a tree. I am not frightened. All of a sudden, a killer whale floats by and goes down the hillside.

A flood represents overwhelming emotions, moving from one phase to another but with emotional ties. The cars floating away symbolize all the difficulties that I have faced with Sam that will be resolved. The tree symbolizes my connection to my home and holding on to what brings me security. The killer whale is my feelings of acceptance for my situation with the house, even though it scares me.

I am still in my home but am living in limbo. Sam hasn't sold the house yet. I feel better about my situation because Sam and I are talking again. Namah has been less involved in my affairs. Sam has moved out of Namah's and now lives closer to the kids.

I trust God knows what He is doing in my life, even though I don't understand why everything played out the way it did. If anything, it gives Sam a chance to set things right between us. Only time will tell. I do wish Sam the best and hope that he can forgive me for the pain I have caused him.

As for my final prayer, I pray that everyone who was effected by the divorce, our friends and family, that we all heal and grow. May we all see this as a fresh new start in our own lives, turn our weaknesses into strengths, and our fear into love.

The Poetry

Serve God also with your bad impulses, then you will serve Him wholeheartedly. - Kabbalah

Set Your Sights Higher

my heart is starting to soften
i'm not dwelling on
the jezebel
that broke up
my marriage
or imagining ways
i would love to
see her suffer

these days
my thoughts are changing
uplifting me, inspiring me
God sent me a dream
and His message was clear:
set your sights higher

One of My Kind

i got use to him
telling me to stay quiet
around his kind
don't bring up God
or aliens or demon attacks
or anything weird

what i heard him say was:
don't be you
don't make me uncomfortable
be the woman
i wish you were-
one of my kind

Blame

it was so naive of him
to think that his drinking
and late so-called business meetings
wouldn't be the cause
of him feeling distant from me

i was at home
i always was
i never went anywhere
sleepless nights
of waiting up for him
cold dinners eaten alone
screaming, crying kids
to attend to
and where was he?

Pins and Needles

it's a very good thing
he left me
i'm not walking on
pins and needles
anymore
the sound of his voice
use to stop my heart
in a terrible, dreadful way
when i was the target
of his anger

like a good woman
i took it
it's a very good thing
i did

i only saw the monster
in him after he left
and he blamed me for
everything that was
wrong with his life

My Own Voice

i wanted to find
my own voice
i realize now
that the only way
to do that
was by divorcing him

he ended up giving me what i always wanted

Lightning in A Jar

he has a wild spirit
about him
i knew this when i
married him

how does one put
lightning in a jar?
i should have known better

Three Rules of Divorce

there should be three simple
rules in divorce if there
is proof of infidelity:
number one, the cheaters pay alimony
number two, you get a free pass
if you beat up your cheating spouse's whore
and number three, the cheating spouse
walks away with nothing

Ugly

divorce is ugly
and so is the woman
he left me for

Drawing

i can't draw worth crap
but i would love to leave
an outline of my fist
on her face

Not My Problem

i laughed
when his business partner
texted me
begging me
to let him move back home

he can't stand her
and is sick of her

all i could think
was not my problem

Envy

she hates me
because deep down
she knows
he will never
give her the life
that he gave me

Grateful

dear Namah,
thank you for
all the inspirational thoughts
you gave me
a lot of them
late at night

i wrote them all down
so I could warn
other women
that their marriage
could be in danger too
seeing as there are
many desperate women
like you
out there
who are godless
and completely ignorant
of God's seventh commandment:
thou shall not commit adultery

Self Love

i definitely can identify
with my anger
i see now
those parts of me
that were screaming out
to be loved
and he never did

with him gone
i am free now
to give those parts
of myself
the love they desperately wanted

Surrender

i started on a journey
up a mountain
at the peak
i looked down
and saw all
the devastation below
so i kneeled down
closed my eyes
and prayed

Love's A Sick Game

here it is
i love two men
one whom doesn't
even acknowledge i am alive
and the other
wishes i was dead
love is a sick game

A Dead Thing

i wonder how long
it will be
while i sit here
that someone will notice
my rage bottled up
inside of me
sure i am quiet now
but wait around awhile
and you will see the flames
burn a hole right through me
no one here notices the secret
hate i bare for him and his jezebel
unless you've been betrayed
like me
and left like a dead thing

Obedience

daily you said
i love you
and i believed you
but i see now
that you loved me
for what i could
do for you
like a slave girl
obeying her master
i obliged

Oppressed Rage

i must confess
that i hate
the both of you
for trying to destroy me
so pardon me
for wanting
to punch
you both
in the face

Reborn

you've added
color to my life
since you left
my black and white existence
suddenly brought to life

Pieces

it wasn't all
all once that
i lost you
it was in pieces
a piece to each woman
you cheated on me with
and then like a crack
in a mirror
you shattered

Should have Known Better

the way you left me
explains why i never
wholeheartedly
gave myself to you
it was the sixth sense
in me when we met
that you were already gone

Snakes

often he apologized
to me
for his cruelty
dishonesty
bigotry
infidelity
how those words
i am sorry
just slipped
off his tongue
snakes are good
at slithering
and slipperiness
i should of
seen the resemblance sooner

Band-Aids

everything in me
hurts
when he left
a thousand wounds
ripped open
inside of me
each day i
tend to one of them
and am careful
not to rip back open
the ones i've bandaged

The Two Don't Mesh

he didn't want
to live in my world
of prayer
meditation
yoga and God
he preferred
his world
of whores
alcohol
marijuana
and money for shiny things

Useless Advice

advice doesn't help
a divorcing woman
unless you've lived
through it
your words are like
water
that nothing can be
built on
send her prayers instead

Invisible

i crawled into bed
and threw
the covers over my head
i tried to make myself
invisible
if i was invisible,
so would be my problems
it didn't work

Your Face

your face
alone
makes me
want to
throw
and break
something

How You Left

it wasn't wrong that
you left, we were broken
it was how you did it:
with a jezebel,
an attorney,
a hidden agenda
to take everything
i built with you
away from me
and give it all
to another woman

The Boy You Still Are

i remember the days of spontaneous road
trips to Mexico and the salty margaritas on
the beach. we'd then head back to the hotel,
roll a joint, and fuck. i think back on those
times and i know we were just kids. now i
am an adult and alcohol, marijuana, and sex
just doesn't do it for me anymore. but you
still hold on to your childlike ways. you've
never been good at letting things go that no
longer serve you. even though it appears
you left me behind, my image will always
haunt you. because you will be forced to
recognize the woman i am and the boy you
still are.

Too Hard to Love

i know you weren't meant for me. you could never listen to my poems i wrote. you could never make time for me and sit down to watch a tv show i liked. you could never finish a conversation with me without the phone ringing and you'd answer it. you could never just hold me without asking what's wrong when nothing was wrong. i just wanted to be held. i know you weren't meant for me because it was too hard for you to love me.

Forgiving Myself

i admit that i held on to you for too long. i
should have left you the first time you
cheated on me. you felt guilty when you
called to tell me what happened. the sincere
apology i heard in your voice. i forgave you.

the second time, i should have left you. i
found her panties underneath your car seat.
fuck i am dumb to of believed you the first
time when you said it would never happen
again.

the third time, i should have left you. you
told me you were in love with her. i said
perhaps i could love her too. fuck i am an
idiot to think that you would ever be satisfied
with just me.

the fourth time, you left me. you lied and
said we needed time apart. but when you
left, you went straight to her. your actions
are unforgivable. and i have to forgive
myself for letting you treat me like anything
less than the goddess i am.

My Position on You

My position on you is this:

You're a coward hiding behind text
messages.
A fraud simply because a lot of parts of you
are fake.
A jezebel because you seduced a married
man.
A liar because in court you lied about the
damn earring.
A thief because nothing of mine belongs to
you.
You're a no good for nothing, evil, conniving,
piece of shit human being.

But that is only my opinion.

Boyish Ways

he was so capable
of being a great husband
i wanted him
to capture my heart
but i was always
ahead of him
he could not
let go
of his boyish ways

My Gratitude to the Other Woman

Thanks for filing an assault charge
on me
my public defender
smeared your deceitful face
in court

Thanks for the public humiliation
on facebook
all those pics of you with my husband
and my kids
only made you look like
a treacherous woman

Thanks for retaining my husband's attorney
it forced me to hire Faith (yes that is her real name)
and fight back, i would have lost everything
it also made me rely on God 100%
now i am even closer to Him

Thanks for seducing my husband,
the man i gave nearly two decades
of my life to,
it took him leaving me
to realize i deserve better
and i will not settle for anything less
than being treated like the goddess
I AM.

Self Worth

i was tired of his shit
a long time ago
but i put up with it
and now i ask myself
why did i?
i didn't have to
no one forced me
to stay
it wasn't love
that kept me
with him
because i see
now that i didn't
love myself
enough to leave him

Nothing

the all i gave
ended up being
nothing
the joy i once felt
now just a bitter
stream of tears
replaced with anger
years and years i gave
years and years you
took from me
and what's left
is a broken woman
with broken dreams
and a jaded smile
to hide my pain

One Shoot

there are no second
chances with me
if you break my heart
chances are i will forgive you
but i didn't give you my heart
in the beginning to break it
i gave it to you to hold

Opposite Directions

i've been watching you
over the years
stumble over
your own feet
going in circles

you've been watching me
over time
moving in a straight line
forward
never looking back
and us falling
further apart

Broken Promises

he promised you a dream
and delivered
instead to you
a hellish nightmare

The Two Fires

i don't know exactly when i became your
victim. did you think i would just lie down
like a dog and let you kick the shit out of
me!? this proves that you never did know
me. for in me is a fire that burns like the
fires of hell or a fire that burns like the sun
in paradise. you discovered what truth i was
for you when you left me for dead.

The Birth of the Warrior

i saved myself from you, or rather you
forced me to. all the weaknesses that you
pointed out in me are now unbreakable and
stronger than your will when you left me. so
i want to thank you for all the hatred you
gave me. all the sticks and stones that you
threw at me, and not one broken bone. your
severity, cruelty, harshness forced the
warrior that was in me to emerge. the scars
she wears from her battle will remind you of
the devoted wife you mistook for your
victim.

A House of Cards

i cried the entire night
i could not sleep
i paced the floor
trying to make sense
of why you left me
for her
how could you destroy
almost two decades
of what we built:
with tears,
dying confessions,
secret regrets,
hopes and dreams-
a life built by TWO
and in a single moment
DESTROYED

was she worth it?

No Courtesy

i felt nothing
when I saw you
no love, no anger, no horror, no regret
i didn't even recognize you
you put on weight
your skin pale
like a ghost
you tried to smile
but it was rushed and forced
i searched your eyes
for an ounce of
shame or guilt
but couldn't find any
but there you were
holding her hand
and still married
to me

A New Awareness Emerging

i locked myself
in my house
i had no intention
of leaving and no
intention of letting
anyone in
i prayed to God
the sun would not
rise the next day
that i would die
and i wouldn't
have to face the
fact our marriage
was over, my world
as i knew it was over
because for so long
you were my world
i didn't know how
i would live without you

but the sun did rise
and slowly my eyes
are adjusting to the light
that now fills the empty
space of your absence

My Body's Reaction to You

i hate you! my mouth hates you and wants
to take back all the *i love yous.* my eyes
hate you and can't stand the sight of you.
my arms and legs hate you and the thought
of having ever wrapped themselves around
you. my vagina hates you and your penis!
every bone, muscle, cell in my body hates
you and screams, *don't come near us you
piece of shit!*

Moving On

it's been a year and a half, and i am still
grieving you. i have not accepted this lose. i
am so tired of being sad and missing the
good parts of you. i try to trick my heart by
focusing on the bad parts, but i cannot fool
her. i tell her this isn't healthy for me
anymore. i want to bury your memory for
good. i picked out a good spot in the
backyard, next to your beloved dog. i think
this is the best thing for the both of us. it's
not good for me to carry around your bones
anymore.

Depression

it felt like i was
packing up my life
and i was forced to start over
my kids' lives torn apart,
our lives torn apart

there's a big hole in me
nothing can fill it

every morning
i hear the birds singing to me
outside the window
as the sun greets me
with a smile

i don't have the strength
to smile back

So Much for So Little

i hate how you
treated me
looking back
i just wanted
you to see
how much
i loved you
i took all your
twisted truths
and half-ass efforts
and still I gave my all
to a man that
did not appreciate
me or my effort
to make us work

Longing to Smile

i can't remember the last time a man has
made me smile. it doesn't take much to
make me smile. i've been so sad for so long,
i think i forgot how to smile. i can force a
smile, but it wouldn't be the same. i
daydream of a guy bringing me flowers, a
lovely bottle of red wine, writing me love
notes. that would make me smile.

he use to tell me i have a beautiful smile. i
wonder if he misses it.

Burying the Dead

my mind
is a
graveyard
of
buried
memories
of you

Growing Stronger Day by Day

i'm in the
best possible
place i can be in
after going
through a
really bad divorce
i look in the mirror
and i really admire
the woman i am becoming

Gone for Good

dear ex-husband,
have you figured
out what you lost yet?
and are you happy
with your decision?

The Heaviness of Mom's Absence

the space
at the table
is empty
where she once sat
her placemat
marks her space
it reminds me
she does still dwell here
if not her body
her heart
if not her words
her memory
if not her smiling eyes
her humor
there is a space
at the table
that is hers
and anyone who sits
here will feel it

Jewels

as the rain
jewels the window pane
i think of our wedding day
it was cold and wet
with a welcoming heart
on that day
i became your wife
you became my husband
as the years passed together
we suffered each other patiently
we were growing apart and no longer wanted
the same things
i did my best to make you happy
you did the best you could to survive your
unhappiness with me
we delayed the inevitable knowing sooner or
later you would leave
i tried to get you to stay
i now know I should of let you go a long time
ago
maybe we would still be friends
maybe we could of at least stand to be in the
same room together
maybe I wouldn't feel the way I do about
you
since your long leaving
i have been bruised and badly battered
by your unkindness, trickeries, and lies

the tears come like flood waters
they are now the jeweled memories of my
enemy

Rejoice While You Burn

this divorce has been hell
but i've discovered
a few things about myself:
i'm stronger than i thought
and i can bend my unpleasant thoughts
to happy ones

i imagine my life
ten years from now
and i have all the success
i desire as a writer
because during the toughest period
in my life
i found my voice

what if instead of suffering, i am happy? will i still be able to write? i think about how my pain has created such heartfelt poems that so many women can relate to. we all ache from a broken heart. we're all just trying to survive this so-called game of life. as this chapter of my life ends, and a new one begins, i can now imagine a life where i am appreciated and truly loved by a man. will this mean the end of me unpacking my thoughts on paper or will it morph into something bigger and grander than i can even imagine for myself? as i leave the last of my parting words to you, i hope i have inspired you to believe in yourself and to move forward in life with courage. always remember, fear is the only true enemy. not your ex-lover that broke your heart. let go of the blame, guilt, and your pride; and surrender to an unconditional love that only you can give yourself. then the right man will come along. i promise.

The Divorcing Woman's Tool Box

AHCCCS Arizona: Medical and Nutrition Assistance. www.azahcccs.gov P: 1-855-432-7587. Check your local state government assistance programs.

Al-anon: Families and friends of alcoholics support group nationwide. www.al-anon.org E: wso@al-anon.org

Association of Arizona Food Banks: www.azfoodbanks.org P: 1-800-445-1914. Check your state for nearby food banks.

Book List:

A Beautiful Composition of Broken, R. H. Sin

The Five Love Languages: The Secret to Love that Lasts, Gary Chapman

The Mind Connection, Joyce Meyer

Unseen, Sara Hagerty

When Things Fall Apart, Pema Chodron

Divorce Care: A divorce support group nationwide. www.divorcecare.org P: 1-800-489-7778 E: info@divorcecare.org

University of Phoenix Counseling Services: University of Phoenix Counseling Skills Center, 1625 W. Fountainhead Parkway, Tempe, AZ P: 480-557-2217. Check your local area for pro-bono clinics on college campuses.

YouTube:

Abraham-Hicks @ Abraham-Hicks Publications

Gnostic Teachings @ Gnostic Students

Joyce Meyer @ Christian Peace Broadcast

Recovery from Narcissistic Abuse by Meredith Miller @ Inner Integration

Words of Gratitude

Thank you to all my friends and family who stuck by me and let me vent. Thank you to everyone that prayed for me. Thank you, Dad, for your loving support and home-cooked meals. Thank you, Jesus, for your loving presence throughout the whole ordeal. And thank you, Invisible Lover, for all the strength and love you sent to me through my dreams.

About the Book

shedding the wife
is about a spiritual journey
through divorce
with inner landscapes
of floods and fires
the storm
becomes a catalyst
to self-discovery
this book is
for all women
healing from the wounds
of betrayal, neglect, and/or abuse
and by doing the inner work
empowers us
to let go of the past
and move forward
as a warrior

Made in the USA
Lexington, KY
13 June 2019